The Quest:
In Search of Me

———— ✳ ————

Tricia Gardella

editors@emerald-books.com

BISAC Categories:

BIO000000   BIOGRAPHY & AUTOBIOGRAPHY / General

BIO022000   BIOGRAPHY & AUTOBIOGRAPHY / Women

ISBN: 978-1-954779-62-4

Summary:

It's 2020, and COVID is shutting down our entire world. Your life is not going as planned. Your husband was not supposed to die before you. You were supposed to travel—together. Now, because of COVID, travel is not even an option. Then fate steps in as it often does and you find yourself on a quest that will put you back on the track you were always meant to be on—writing—showing that age need never be a measure of old.

About the Cover Photograph:

"Evolution in progress: great-granddaughter, mother, grandmother, great-grandmother."

Dedicated to...

My special mystery man,

My Write Sisters who took me back after twenty years off track,

And to my dear friends Christine Pedi and Seth Redutsky, whom I have never met.

Introduction

————— ❈ —————

I have to ask. How would you feel if someone you had not seen or even thought of in sixty years came waltzing back into your life—your very quiet life? Oh, did I mention the person was someone whom you professed to love? For almost an entire year. You were seventeen and she was sixteen. Had you even thought of her in all those sixty years?

Has there ever been an age without its war somewhere in the world, down through the history of civilized humanity? I mention this simply to set a place in history. Each of us has one—a place. And even if it's not happening right next door, even if we aren't media addicts, what happens in our universe affects us—sometimes in very surprising ways. Sometimes things happen, because life happens, and for no other reason.

I was born near the end of World War II. It has been a while since I was a hormonal teenager, no matter that most of this COVID time that's exactly how I've been acting. And I've loved every minute of it. Almost. Not that I'm proud of every minute. But what fun it has been for someone who was beginning to believe that twilight years meant, like eventide, that things simply grow darker. And darker.

By March 2020, I had been a widow for three long years, a senior who actually likes alone time: time to write, time to design, time to create, time to go where I want, when I want. And I have always been a believer in fate. How else could my life have been so full of magic? So, when my sister Pam mentioned in passing that her stepson had just bought property belonging to an old high school boyfriend's family, my ears perked up. COVID restrictions had just begun, and I had just canceled my two overseas trips scheduled for that spring. All winter, I had been making rugs from accumulated scraps to get rid of old supplies and to have a project. **Lots** of rugs. I was about rugged out. And while working on a class reunion, I had heard that this particular old beau was living alone and had moved back to California. How hard could it be to find him? Google can find anyone. Right? So, there he was! In seconds. Facebook. Seven listings. But not one of them was him. A glitch. I kept looking.

How the internet had changed in my twenty-year sabbatical from writing! No one can appreciate it more than I, remembering all those days spent researching in a rural library and coming up with less than what can be uncovered on Google in three seconds.

Three days later, I called my sister. "Do you remember where he lives?" She did. I found an address. Let the quest begin.

I stuck a note in the mail and sent it to a house address I had found through Google. I waited. And waited. And waited.

Finally, I called my sister. "Do you think Phil [her husband] might have an email address for him?"

"I'll ask," she said. Two days later, she sent me his email address. I sent another note. And waited. And waited.

Then, one day in May, when I had completely given up hope, I opened my mailbox and there it was.

Hello Tricia, it began. He said it was a "treat" to hear from me, and he sounded pleased that I had written. Then he worried about what I had planned. My letter had teased about us becoming pen pals. He was not sure about such a commitment. "Pen pals, now, I dunno, that may be going too far. My turn, your turn, my turn again till death do us part: not sure about that." But he agreed that a letter or two might work just fine.

An email I had sent him much earlier reached him that same day. So much for the speed of the internet. But to be fair, it seems to have taken the scenic route via Minnesota. The last words that he jotted in his short note wowed me: "On my usual Sunday walk, a most unusual memory showed up—your mother singing 'Panis Angelicus.' So, I listened to her while I walked. Wow!"

He remembered. But remembered me? Not so much.

I sat down and wrote.

The stack of letters from this correspondence.

Letter 1: May 2020

———— ❋ ————

Good morning. My mother *could* sing (to my ear anyway), which makes me quite critical of most sopranos, but I just happened to hear a young woman this weekend—Lauren Michelle—whose talent and voice give me both hope and goosebumps.

I was being facetious when I suggested we be pen pals. Never was a good pen pal, even in grade school, and was so jealous of classmates who stayed connected with others around the world. But "a letter or two" works fine for me, so long as you fill in the holes of your last sixty years. As I mentioned earlier, hearing your name (and because of all the extra time piling up due to this blasted pandemic), I began my quest. My quest for what, I'm not sure. But I love quests. Oh, and did I mention that I am often impulsive?

The last I heard about you was when I was working on a class reunion and digging for information about D—maybe fifteen years ago. Someone, can't remember who, told me you had separated from her and had moved to the desert. Since then, I've discovered your blog, so I feel I have pieced together the real you. But mysteries remain, and I would love for you to fill me in. But from your blog and something I found about your magazine, it seems you have barely changed.

My heart ached when I could feel your continuing grief over your older brother's death. I wanted so much to be able to fix it sixty years ago, and that feeling digs even deeper when I read your praise of him, as though you were so inferior to him. Remember, I knew you both. I loved your blog thoughts on "There" becoming our new "Here." I had never heard it put quite that way. Life is so fickle, but "the what-we-are" remains—sometimes buried—from birth to death.

Your letter to the *New Yorker*, and something about a couple taking over the magazine you had published, came up on Google with an email address. Off went my email. Ages later, I received an answer from them, but was told simply that you were no longer involved. I grew suspicious when the next morning a post popped up in my email with your name in the subject. It was quite strange and had nothing to do with my mission, but I read into it that you may have been sent some information about my quest.

So, I waited. Nothing. Weeks passed. No returned letter. No email. Time to quit? But...might Phil be able to get your email address? He did. Never even asked why. Off went my emails. The silly one about "moving toward our bliss" then the more desperate one about your well-being. Still no word. That was mid-April. I didn't think you were dead, like over half my class of '62, because you were recently named on those escrow papers. But I did picture you in some sort of assisted living. It took well over a month for the original letter I had sent to your home address to come back to me. That was that. I continued reading your blog and wondering. I found passages that mentioned D. One time you call her your wife, then later you call her a friend. Were you still together? I kept telling myself to stop. I didn't listen. One day I said, the heck with this! Blame it on the pandemic.

I called the number I had for D. Remember she was in my class, and I've always organized our reunions. Got the answering machine. It did not sound like I remembered her voice those sixty years ago, so I decided to call it quits. For a day. Then I decided to try just one more time. Answering machine again. I was done. Really done this time. But an hour later my phone rings and a voice asks, "Did you call?"

It was D. We had a great visit, and she shared your proper address. I wrote immediately—and heard nothing. I hate scrapping a mission, but it was obvious this one needed to be scrapped. So, I dove back into my rug-making and reading. (Actually reread *Franny and Zooey*. Do you remember giving that to me?)

Then Thursday I opened my mailbox, and there it was. And like Emily Dickenson, whom you mention many times in your blog, I waited until I was finished with all I needed to do and read. But my mission is not complete. Please tell me about your parents, about your family, about your life.

Now what?

His next letter began with him still thinking about my mother's singing. He wondered (because he had stopped going to church in the seventh or eighth grade) how could something like voice stick in memory for so long? The thing is, my mother sang everywhere in the county. Her voice was at the top of the request list for both weddings and funerals—a beautiful, clear, operatic soprano, the choice of the world back in those days. So glad she lived when she was appreciated.

I had not mentioned my husband in my previous letter, but he knew and asked how long it had been since Jack had passed. Then he began to write more about his brother. His brother died right after he left for college. My dear friend came home a very different man from the boy who had left for college a few weeks earlier. How I wished I could fix his pain. If nothing else, I have never forgotten this.

"Sometimes, with my brother, it seems like he could have gone a week, a month, or only a few days ago," he says. Sixty years and the hurt never changed.

He remembered being home for a visit decades ago and seeing a notice for a benefit that was coming up "for one of your children," and he hoped all my kids were alive and well. How could he not have known my daughter had died a few months after that? How could anyone not know?

It seems his father died around that same time. I had not heard, and I lived in the same county—a small county at that. Maybe I didn't know because it was around the same time our Gina was dealing with her issues. I remember noticing at the time how the world kept turning, no matter what I was going through.

His mother remained up here for a time after his dad died. Then she moved down to be closer to her son and his children. Soon, she was doing "much-needed" secretarial work for his magazine. She died a week before her ninetieth birthday.

A few years after that, he reconnected with an old classmate. They fell in love. He went to live with her and her three children somewhere in the far north. This was after his involvement with a woman who had been managing a complicated medical problem. They had met in graduate school. He became her caregiver until she died. He misses her still.

"Some dead folks have a way of sticking around forever, I swear," he writes.

He seems to realize that he has been talking a lot about the dead when he writes, "Okay, just one more thing about dead people…" And he asks if there seemed to be any number-one cause for the passing among all my classmates? I had mentioned in my previous letter the high percentage lost. He had played football with many of them.

He didn't remember giving me Franny and Zooey.

Letter 2: May 2020

— ✻ —

It didn't have to be when you were in grammar school that you last heard my mother sing. She sang at most funerals and weddings in the county, as well as other events, and trained with Mrs. Swansea for many years.

Jack died late New Year's night 2018. Our oldest daughter died fifty years ago in February; my brother Ted and Mom died in the mid-seventies of hypertrophic cardiomyopathy (HCM). I was diagnosed a short time later—and here I am. Makes one wonder. I have passed it along to my son, and he shared it with his two children. That can sometimes play with one's head, but three of us have defibrillators, and I'm guessing Angela will get hers soon. I was one of the ICD [implantable cardio defibrillator] pioneers. I have had mine for more than thirty years.

I also have two daughters, seven grandchildren (six boys, one girl—all born within three years), one great-grandson, and his sister Piper, born last week, with one more great coming in July. My youngest three grandchildren are twenty-three. Yikes. No wonder I feel a bit old. Sometimes it is difficult for me to believe I was that age when we discovered Gina had cancer. I would never wish that on anyone.

Then again, I would not give up one minute, or a single experience, from those days. They taught me to live. Oh, did I mention I was six months pregnant with my third when Gina was diagnosed? She was two. And she was my oldest. She was three years and nine months old the day she died. A year later, her brother was born. I have a five-generation picture of my great-grandfather, my grandfather, my mother, me, and Gina. I have been the only one left from that photo for forty years.

Did you finish grad school? I finally earned my BA in Ancient History and Classical Archaeology. Only took me fifty-five years. But I was busy. Something drove me to learn to do it all. My goal was always to be able to do everything that earlier humans could do. But how could I not, having such things as a vacuum, toilet, dishwasher? Those objects of convenience made it easier for me to pretend. I taught myself all the home arts. Even had a milk cow for a time, but we didn't need that much butter, and she played havoc with my allergies.

I won't bore you with the various businesses I began (then grew bored with) over the years. Maybe another time. But when I turned forty, I decided it was time for me. I had always wanted to write. A couple years later, I sold my first book to Harper and Row. (Remember, this was in the old days.) I thought I had it made. Harper and Row became Harper Collins that year. My editor, who had been at Harper and Row for eighteen years, left. And I was orphaned. It took five years for me to sell my next book. This time, not only did I lose my editor, I lost my Macmillan imprint, and then I lost my contract. But I got to keep the advance. Several years later, they wanted it back and I told them my father was a judge and he said I didn't have to return it. That was that.

It took another five years for me to sell that book again. This time to Houghton Mifflin. My last book to be published was to yet another publisher. It came out the year we bought the building in Jamestown—where I would spend my next sixteen years.

Opening a store was never on my list. But the building was a looker, and it was being auctioned on Saturday. I thought it would be perfect for our children. Here's where I need to tell you that John [my son] married the youngest daughter of the Columbia Candy Kitchen Nelsons. I fantasized that half the store would make a perfect Candy Kitchen satellite and my daughters would run an ice cream parlor on the bar side. *Wrong.* The Candy Kitchen had already opened two stores in three years and had no desire for more. My daughters had very small children and no desire for such a commitment. Besides which, Jodi and family were still living in Idaho, though they moved back down that year.

We bid on the building anyway...and got it.

I decided an ice cream parlor on the bar side and a gift shop featuring local crafters on the other side would work great. I would set things up, hire people, and keep on writing. *Wrong.* But this was probably a good thing for my life. You know how writers live so much in their heads? This brought me back home again.

It took time, but the business grew, often taking its own turns. It helped that it just happened to be in a tourist town smack in the middle of California Gold Country. Pretty soon, I no longer thought of writing.

All my creative juices were going into the zillion things I wanted to make for the store. It took me sixteen years to burn out this time. On leap year day 2016, I walked out, handing most of my inventory over to one of my cooks. Not the best business sense—but so freeing.

Spent the next two years traveling and trying to reshape the home front, which had suffered sixteen years of neglect. And I organized our fifty-five-year reunion, the best we had ever had—we had all mellowed so. Life was great!

Except for that damn cough.

It had been there since we had arrived home from Europe that past spring. No other symptoms. I thought about you and wondered if he had COPD? What I really thought was that he probably had something like chronic bronchitis. I made an appointment at Stanford with a pulmonary specialist, but they couldn't see him until December 4. It was the first of October. On October 10, I told Jack to load up. I was taking him to the ER (at Stanford). That afternoon they removed nearly two liters of fluid from his lung, and we learned he had lung adenocarcinoma with lesions already on his spine and brain. When no one would offer a time frame, I knew it was bad. People sometimes ask if it was the diagnosis that spiraled him down. Not at all. It was more like he had been teetering on the brink, and the balance suddenly shifted. His first words after his diagnosis were, "I thought I'd live to eighty-five." About broke my heart. He made that agonizing time so easy for all of us. If only we could all pass with such dignity.

Then I ran. Got in the car and drove for seven weeks (11,000 miles). After that, I decided to take each of my grandchildren on a trip. Was overseas four times last year. Was booked for a cruise through the Suez Canal (Dubai to Rome) the first of April and should be just getting back from a classical music tour through Poland, the Czech Republic, and Vienna with my sisters. And here I sit.

I'm one who believes many of the best journeys begin with detours. This forced lockdown has been interesting. I'm writing! Nothing newsworthy, but I'm writing! And it is all because of my quest—to learn how and where you are.

Enough. I am rambling. But I just want you to know that your blog has been just what I needed. I have jotted down thoughts about many of your posts. I've tried journaling before, but this has become a different kind of journaling. It won't last. When I was writing, I was prolific. Hard to believe, right? I've been clearing out files recently and don't even remember writing half the stories I've dug up.

I smiled when I read your comment, "Some dead folks have a way of sticking around forever, I swear." I had just been grappling with the same thought. In my notes, I wrote, "Why does the loss of some weigh heavier on us than the loss of others?"

I believe each life experience is a chance to learn. No matter what you think, your time with that classmate you cared for until her end was not about you replacing your brother. It was about you, who you are. Some people take a long time to see, some never do. Those we have loved and lost live on...through us. Everyone I have ever truly cared for becomes a part of the ever-changing me.

I haven't actually calculated the percentage of classmates lost, but it is great, and I see no single cause. Drugs, alcohol, cancer, heart, stroke, Vietnam, Alzheimer's—all are represented. Alzheimer's is the one that grips my gut. My dad and grandfather both died from it. Maybe not *from* it, but with it.

I enjoyed reading *Franny and Zooey* even more this time around—this time, for obvious reasons, feeling more of a connection with Mrs. Glass.

This letter fills your "couple of letters" criterion. But I want to know more—about your children, about your magazine, about your choice of the desert. And are you going north this summer?

Five generations together

Graduation: University of Leicester 2019

I was quite pleased when he agreed to more "pitching and catching." Thus began our back-and-forth about what he saw as a difference between letters and books. This was a through line of our entire correspondence. He would say that when writing a book, you have only one person to worry about—yourself, while writing a letter, the writer has two people to think about. This never made sense to me. I am a writer. It makes no difference whether I am writing a letter or a book. I always write for me.

He was now living alone, a long way from his partner. But I had been dealing with a growing concern. Was I trying to squeeze in somewhere I did not belong? One short sentence from D, stuck in the middle of this particular letter, seemed to be meant to ease my concerns, I think. But in many ways, it confused me more. "Tell Tricia we are best friends." He had obviously discussed me with her. Did this mean there was room for another friend? I hoped so.

In this letter, I learned that we shared more than the love of literature. He told me about his "wonky" heart and that he had a pacemaker. Could there be a better description for an out-of-whack heart than wonky? I unashamedly stole his description and use it often. Why had I never thought of it?

His letter ends talking about how he had mellowed toward Thoreau after learning that he, too, had a brother who had died too early. In his arms. From lockjaw! And he wondered if this was why Thoreau became a recluse and went off to Walden Pond. Always about his brother.

18

Letter 3: May 2020

———— ❖ ————

How can you always be so wrong? Only one person to think about in a novel, two in a letter? Makes no difference. A pitcher always pitches to a catcher. Even if that catcher is simply the pitcher. But a novel takes planning, focus, intelligence. That's why I never write them. Letter-writing is more like diarrhea. A way to relieve pressure. No rhyme, no reason, simply relief. Or guilt. Or some combination of the two.

Bless D. You are simply best friends? I'm feeling the teensiest bit better.

You mention anger in one of your blogs and I wondered. Now I see that you too are familiar with the irrational drive of the quest. You actually tried to contact the only survivor of the crash that killed your brother? We think we will find satisfaction, peace. Do we? More often, it just seems to stir up anxiety. Yes, we do need closure, which I'm not sure we ever truly get. But can you imagine what you might be going through if you were the only one to survive such a crash? Forgive him. That should close a tiny bit more of that *huge* hole in your heart.

I've always thought I was the supreme guilt-donkey. I feel blame for everything. But I think you have me beat by a mile. Not only do you feel guilt for surviving your brother, but now you feel guilty for an attempted contact with his survivor. *Live!* We all die in our time: two minutes to 110 years. You see your military enlistment after college as a chance to self-sacrifice? And you were newly married? How could you choose to whom you owed your allegiance? Your late brother? Your new wife? Yourself?

Twenty-seven beats per minute and you were still conscious? You have a good heart. Pacemakers. We have something in common. It's when my heart rate gets around two hundred beats for more than seventeen seconds that my troubles begin. Only happened once for medical reasons. Should have died the day after Thanksgiving in November 2008. But I was already quite familiar with that erupting-volcano feeling of a defibrillator. Mid-2001 they replaced the batteries in my defibrillator but didn't notice the faulty lead. A few days later, my device went off. Fired fifteen times in three hours before they turned it off. Thought it was going to kill me.

You did write about Thoreau in your blog and compared his feelings with those of Brigham Young (I think) who also lost a brother. My brother Ted was working on his PhD at Stanford when he died—sudden death. I often wonder what he might have accomplished.

Describe the mature you. Do you still have that enigmatic smile? Those beautiful long fingers? Long hair? Or short? A paunch? I truly cannot imagine how you might appear today.

Just as I can never imagine Gina at 54. They amputated her arm at two. She was paralyzed from the waist down before she was three, and she couldn't talk at the end because of a huge tumor in her vocal cords. But that is not what I remember. When I picture her, I see that smile, those bright brown eyes, and her cheerfulness—no matter how terrible the circumstance. *She* carried me.

Remember my good friend Sally? If I remember right, we double-dated a couple times. Did you know that she and I had kittens at my house named Esteban and Eduardo? Learned that from one of my college letters to Jack. Esteban disappeared when I was in college. Have no idea what happened to Eduardo. Hard to believe that Sally and Ed have both been gone close to ten years. (Was just feeding my kitten and it brought back memories.) Ed was mine before hers, one of three men I have loved my entire life—no matter that I dumped him when we entered high school. What a treasure I was.

I have a confession to make. I sometimes love music more than words. How could humanity survive without each of them? Without one single word, oh, what a musician with vision can 'say'! The feeders of my soul seem to be classical piano, flamenco guitar, and some solo violin. A nourished soul 'sees' much clearer. Where does talent come from? Why didn't I get more? Now I simply appreciate. Then along comes Plotinus in my reading today. I felt an immediate connection. He too felt "the beauty of things perceived by the senses." Isn't this what this life, this greatest gift we will ever get, is all about?

Often I would write (and send) two or more letters while waiting. Getting back to me never seemed to be at the top of his list. What can I say? I'm a producer.

Letter 4: May 2020

———◆❋◆———

Here's the problem. I agree that there is a need for two: pitcher and catcher. But what if the pitcher feels driven to throw even when the catcher is not ready to catch? In a ballgame, a catcher can simply ignore most wild pitches, unless there are runners on base. Then again, why can't I wait for my pitches to be caught and returned? Because I'm a pitcher and have to pitch when I have to pitch, or I will go nuts. And why am I making you deal with my wild pitches? Well, you did publish a letter-writing magazine. Did you ever have articles on writing etiquette? Maybe you should send me a copy.

You can throw these letters away, but I feel compelled to write them. (When will this lockdown end?) Of course, this doesn't explain why I have to send them. But I do. There are simply things I want to say when I think about them.

Maybe this is the result of a box of letters I recently dug out. I knew they were there. I put them there more than fifty years ago. I wrote Jack nearly every night for the year I was away at college. I remember nothing, and what have I discovered? I

23

am little more than a sixteen-year-old in a seventy-five-year-old's body. Is this what senility is about?

Then what did I do? I looked up my college roommate whom I hadn't seen in much of that same fifty years. She lives a whole hour away. We had both dropped out of school to get married that same summer. Our fellas had gotten along great. But life happens. We have already gotten together for lunch twice, with the requisite social distancing, of course.

It makes me sad that the new generations will never have those dusty boxes of ancient letters to dig up. Most likely there is more back-and-forth in this day, but it's all electronic—nothing lasting. Sad for historians. Sad for the aged.

Today I was thanking you for introducing me to Leonard Cohen. I had heard of him, of course, but I had never *heard* him. I love YouTube! And I like him. A lot!

Are you familiar with the Alan Parsons Project? A band out of England. I listened to "Limelight" today for the first time in years. It used to be my personal anthem, and because of some of your blog comments, I'm thinking it might be a good one for you. Now that I have discovered all that is available on YouTube, I may never get another thing done. Except writing letters.

I've been wondering about you in Vietnam and why you had to go? Jack received his summons the day Kennedy signed the bill that married men could no longer be drafted. Weren't you married around that time?

Like Thoreau (and others you bash), I am pretty much a loner. I enjoy being alone with my thoughts. I love being home–until they tell me I have to be. Two years ago next month, I was headed to Washington state to visit friends. The day before I was due to leave, I went into a-fib, a common development of HCM and age. It had not been that uncommon for me, but rarely lasted much longer than fifteen minutes. After four hours, I called Stanford. A couple hours later, I canceled my trip. I remained in a-fib 24/7 for the next two months. Five cardioversions, an ablation, medication changes—nothing worked. I could barely make it from my bed to my chair. I couldn't read, I couldn't watch TV, I couldn't even listen to music. For two months! Then one September morning, I woke up and I was back. Just like that!

That morning, I decided I was doing whatever I want to when I want to for as long as I can. Because I can. Sounds as though I am an invalid, but actually I am in pretty good shape, just defective. In oh-so-many ways.

Been even better this year, and I'm thinking it may be because when they changed my ICD last fall, they connected both pacemakers (ventricle and atrial). Whatever the reason, I like it. I would rather be dead than live as a zombie.

Okay, I have to ask. Are you and D a couple or not? In my arguments with myself – to write or not to write – I wonder how I would feel if some idiot of the opposite sex was writing to my spouse? I know how Jack would have felt.

"I'm so sorry for the loss of your firstborn. Oh my. Oh my. I hadn't known," his letter began. Then he pointed out how some claim that grief is a function of genetic possibilities gone awry. He talks about a mother's grief being greater than a father's because of a mother's limited reproduction possibilities. Maybe it was something I had eaten that day, but for some reason that set me off. He then suggested that his lifelong grieving for his brother fits such a pattern because he died "in the prime of his possibilities for reproduction."

He then described his father taking him aside shortly before he was due to ship off for Vietnam. His father wanted a grandchild. "I was dumbfounded at the time," he said. "You mean my seed is more important than me?"

Next, he went into the difference between letters and books. Again. Book culture, as he sees it, "had become too lopsided, unbalanced, with just a few writers and millions of readers," which leads us to lose "sight of one another."

Then, in his next paragraph, he admitted he has been lately "back-sliding, enjoying the great freedoms that books bring, their distance, their remove from the things of time." Once again, we were on the same page.

From there, he jumped into Jedediah Smith, the early American explorer, entangling himself "all too much in the things of time," and wondered, "Do you entangle yourself all too much in the things of time?"

If he only knew.

His next jump went to my children or grandchildren. Did any of them have imaginary playmates?

Letter 5: June 2020

———— ❃ ————

I need to read this book on evolutionary psychology (the thought of which is making me quite crabby at the moment).

We grieve because our loved one isn't going to perpetuate our genes? Really? What a terrible way to think of it. Yet when I rein in my emotions, I can see some merit to this argument. John Joseph Gardella IV (Jack) has a baby coming in a few weeks. They didn't want to know the gender until the baby gets here. And I am literally aching that it will be a boy. Why? Because he is the only one who can hand down the family name. So, I do care about this perpetuation, but not for genetic reasons. In fact, I'm praying the baby skips right over a few of the genes it is my fortune to hand on. Of course, I will adore whatever gender. Does this go back to evolutionary psychology? I don't think so. It is nothing more than self-centered hope. And the weird thing is, it's not even my family name. But it is my family's name. Make sense?

Forgive me. It's simply timing. Just finished reading *The Great Influenza: The Deadliest Pandemic in History.* Can you imagine the grief of that era? With both pandemic and war? (And we think we are the only ones!) It's always words that carry me through trying times. The ones I read. The ones I write. My father was a reader. I remember him reading snippets from *Reader's Digest* to my mother while she was making dinner, and this one has stuck with me through time: "Life is what happens while you are making other plans." Words I live by every day. A couple nights ago, a character on a program I was watching said, "People plan, and God laughs." (I heard it on *The Practice* but have since learned it is an old Jewish saying.) Once again, words put things into perspective.

In one of your blog posts, you ask, "Has literacy stunted our growth?" How can you even think such a thing? How do you load your toilet paper when you are loading a new roll? Over? Under? In an assignment for a public-speaking class I was taking, I argued that glass-half-empty people load their rolls with the paper draping down the back. To my mind literature (words) fertilizes growth. It encourages us to think. It helps us to remember. Of course, for this to work, "meanings of words must be fixed, at least for a time, since otherwise no assertion is definite." Read these words yesterday in Bertrand Russell's *History of Western Philosophy*. I'm taking them out of context to remind myself how much we need definite assertion at times.

When Gina was dying, how I read. And read. And read. Never did find an answer. So many opinions. Do you ever wonder if we don't analyze things to death?

I load my toilet paper over the top.

29

Of course your father wanted a grandchild. From you! Like my grandson, only *you* could forward *your* family line, your family name. Your seed was not more important than you. It was simply an extension of you. Something tangible he would have if—God forbid—he lost you.

As I write, I feel my emotions relaxing. But I still bristle at the concept of my grief being nothing more than a "function of genetic possibilities." The definition of grief is "deep sorrow," which can be felt for so many reasons besides death. At the moment, I am grieving that Leonard Cohen died before I "knew" him. (Nothing to do with genetics.) He was so cute (sexy) for an old man. And that gravelly voice...WOW!

Do you have any copies of your magazine or know where I might get one? I would love to understand your crusade. Books and letters give us such different things. How can we not escape into books when we have nowhere else to go? I tried the sleuth books you talked about. Can't do 'em. But I did just discover a "new" (older than me) author, Noah Gordon, who writes my favorite genre—historical fiction. I devoured his nine books in a week. And cried when there were no more.

Do you ever wake up with words flowing through your mind? I've been listening to a lot of Alan Parsons of late. This morning, it's "Time flowing like a river. Time flowing to the sea. Who knows when we will meet again, if ever?"

So, yes, to answer your question, I want to "entangle myself in the things of time." (There is never enough time.) But lately I find there is way too much time. And though I have plenty I could be doing to fill this void, I find I do not want to. I want to drive!

I was thinking of driving up to Washington State in a couple weeks. Have a number of friends up that way. But there is way too much pandemic turmoil up there at the moment. *Sigh.*

I do remember one of our evenings together. To be honest, I have probably romanticized it through the years. You brought me home from our date, then we decided you should come back later, and we would meet by our pool. The memory surprises me because what I remember most about you is the feeling that you were afraid that I (because I was such a wild child?) was going to corrupt you and that you weren't quite sure how to prevent it. (You talked about that a lot.) But no matter. You came back that night and we sat there. On the chaise. In the moonlight. And talked. I have no idea why we made such an arrangement. My parents would not have cared one bit if we had sat out there until the sun rose. So long as I was home.

I don't remember talking behind Raney's—or *didn't*. But something stirs. I do have a hazy memory of us in St. Anne's memorializing your brother.

To answer your question, none of my kids or grandkids had imaginary friends. Maybe because they had siblings or cousins so close in age. My girls never played much with dolls. Maybe ranch life makes things different. Though my girls have never been much of what you might call ranchers. They did what they had to. Period. But John could not have been more of what his father hoped for if Dad had blueprinted him himself.

Thank God I have him. And now his son, Jack, who had never shown much interest in ranching (and has a degree in accounting), has decided he wants to ranch! John is elated! Good things do come to those who wait.

What do your children do? Do you see them often? I am so spoiled. All of mine will be living on this ranch as soon as Jodi gets her house built. They've just broken ground. Four of my grands also live right here. Two others live nearby. Only one is away. He's an apprentice lineman and just called to tell me that he starts a new job in Butte, Montana, tomorrow. He's been in Moab. I think he has another year to finish, then will probably look for a job around here.

Do you ever worry about being polluted? I think that is why I avoid people. I need my world full of wonder and wondering. Not that everything has to be all bright lights and happy faces. But there is so much stupidity, so much negativity, out there. I no longer watch the news. I don't want to know. I like people. When my kids and grandkids played sports and when I had my store, I had just the right amount of contact with people. I guess you might call me a private person—very private. Group thinking makes me angry. Why I left the church. Why I dropped out of organizations.

And then there is Emily Dickenson. I get it. I want to think what I think, feel what I feel, without outside interference, too. But I think the letter Emily is reading in the poem you included is from someone she cares about. Remember, this is from a female viewpoint. As usual with me and poetry, the last two lines have me wondering.

Tell me more about your letter-writing crusade. How many years did you spend? Tell me more about the M experience. Was she a letter writer? I'm so sorry it had to end with her death.

Do books really bring freedom? Guess it depends what you read. Last week, I was so hopeful, so free. This week, I'm carrying the weight of the world. But look what I've been reading. Then you throw in evolutionary psychologists. *Geesh*. Now I <u>have</u> to read about them too.

And you are wrong about a mother's grief being greater. I saw my husband cry twice—when we were told Gina had cancer and when we were told he had cancer. Much, much deeper the first time.

You seem to remember so much of what you read. And I am jealous! I have read thousands of books, yet the sum total of what I remember wouldn't fill one. So frustrating. Have you ever written for publication, aside from letters? If not, why not? You could have added another name to that lopsided writer/reader equation you are always talking about You do realize how few read? I am, however, thinking the number of those listening to books is increasing. Does that count?

Tricia and Gina on the Christmas before Gina's passing

Letter 6: June 2020

———— ❄ ————

Still flogging myself for yesterday's letter. It's the grief/genetic equation, I'm guessing. What happens when we attempt to analyze human emotion using science? Some things should be left alone. Like grief. Everyone's is different.

You and I approach things so differently. I've been thinking this is why I should not be so quick to respond to your letters. I need to read them over and over until I understand what you *might be* saying. My take on something is visceral. Yours is logical. I don't get logic. I didn't get it in college, and (so far) that section is the only part of Russell's book I can't get.

Though I do think most of my decisions are logical. Am I digging a hole here?

It's the intentional concept that gives me pause. Would anyone other than a handful of scientists see grief this way? It's like the argument that viruses mutate because they want to *use* their hosts, not kill them. Probably true, but intentional? Using intention as a reason for any other sort of evolution troubles me. Isn't intention conscious? Deliberate? Calculated? Does the wonder of the development of something like the universe have to be categorized down to that degree? Can I not wonder?

Most of the billions in our world carry the same genes I carry. So why do I care about the genes *I'm* passing down? What I care about is a particular accumulation of genes. A particular person. So often, it is not our progeny that we are grieving, so how can it be considered mourning my genetic possibilities? Who gives a darn about that? As I see it, it simply comes down to grieving the loss of someone you care about, whether you birthed them or not. Your grief is the search for a scientific explanation. Mine is appreciation. They were mine, part of my life, no matter how long their time.

And since I'm writing again, I was thinking about your daughter A and her "friends." One time, I was telling my friend Mary about me telling my mom, when I was five or younger, that I used to be an old man. And Mary pulls out this whole book about very young children relating stories about their "other" mothers or their "other" special friends. It seems children usually forget their others as they grow older. Makes one wonder about imaginary friends?

Also been giving the Emily Dickenson poem you included more thought. Still wondering why Dickenson sighs for "lack of heaven" after claiming how "infinite" she is to "no one that you (we) know." A different kind of heaven than God's heaven. Has she been rejected? You connect this to a desire for privacy. What I see is anticipation, hunger, hope (for fulfillment of what she desires), but it doesn't come. Thus, the lack of heaven, but not religious heaven, she tells us.

I've been bottle-feeding a kitten for the past few weeks. One day it came to me: the driving force of nature is hunger. There are so many kinds of hunger.

Letter 7: June 2020

———— ✳ ————

I'm sending you notes from this weekend. Why? They make me smile. Probably be sorry tomorrow. But it is what it is.

Are my pitches coming too fast? Too furious?

Do heavenly bodies make man less lonely in the universe?

Do you know Leonard Cohen's "Tower of Love"?

You asked the other day if I entangle myself "all too much in the things of time"? If this song doesn't exit my head soon, I will strangle myself in the things of time. On the other hand, I was wishing yesterday that I could go back twenty years. Not that I have anything against this period of my life. I have enjoyed every phase. Was just thinking again about those three books I've always wanted to write. But they require time, which I no longer have.

Been thinking that I'm a better pitcher. You only pitch what you have caught. (Then again, wild pitches can make things difficult.)

Could I have chosen a worse time to read philosophy?

Do you really believe flowers have morals?

Thank you for your help this weekend. Pitching and catching is driving me crazy. I am driving myself crazy. So, I made a decision and began aiming my pitches toward a to-do list. Amazing what got done. Feeling good. For the moment.

Can you tell me where this came from?
"I suspect I'm looking in books not for knowledge but for love. I want to be told how infinite I am." (This was from one of your last blog posts.)

My favorite of your writing: Words "play like puppies in the grass."

Thank you for bringing a smile to my mopping today. The thought—you going overnight from peace march to deployment. And I worry that I am weird?

Got it! I've been envisioning both pitcher and catcher in isolation. Pitch, pitch, pitch. But there is an entire world out there throwing things our way, if we want it or not.

Bertrand Russell reminds me of you. All that intellect peppered with delicious (but subtle) humor.

Been wondering if maybe the new generation doesn't have it right. All the silliness of letters saved for posterity. Is it really a good thing?

Watched almost two hours of logic on YouTube. Still don't get it. Why do I need mathematical equations when words serve so much better? Will we be one day speaking in mathematics?

From *Last Tango in Halifax*: "Words fall out of your mouth onto the floor and want for someone to pick them up." Great sentence!

Are word combinations stronger when accompanied by music?

I don't think I look for myself in books, but I so often see myself and wonder, how do they know?

Even when responding to a letter, we sing of "me," don't you think? Our thoughts are set in motion by what someone else writes, but our response is "our" song. All about us. How we see it.

Do we really *need* someone hearing our words or simply need to imagine someone hearing our words?

I understand passion, for I have always been driven. What I don't always understand is where a passion is placed. My passion at the moment is writing these letters.

My niece lives not too far from where he lives, and since I love to drive, and since I was very curious about him, I figured a short side-trip would fit in just right.

"Dear Tricia, A visit in person wouldn't work for me. Or rather it might, but the odds are fifty-fifty at best."

From the first, I had shared my cellphone number. Suggested texting. Never used. Never commented on. Just as well. I was enjoying the writing. The waiting? Not so much. I don't think I had realized how much I had missed writing. Until then, until our letters.

He wanted to know how I felt about people commenting on what I wrote. To me, positive comments are worth more than money. Could that be because most writers make very little money from what they put to paper? Appreciation is our gold.

As random as they are, he thanks me for all the thinking my letters have stirred up for him.

Letter 8: June 2020

---·❋·---

Thanks! Another thing to fret about. Declining bee populations. No pollen, no letters. A depressing thought.

Looked up evolutionary psychology. Some of it makes complete sense. Other parts, I have a difficult time swallowing. Still haven't run across the part that deals with grief. Maybe my searches need to be more specific. Was introduced to Noam Chomsky on the way, a linguist (aside from being a great thinker). So now I want to know more about the development of language and linguistics. Chomsky claims that language developed in a very short period of time. He says languages change but don't evolve, that language is internal, just used for thinking. What do you think?

Chomsky also mentions bees. He says they have the best communication system in the world. But no one writes about their communication because no one understands it, and it's too difficult to figure out. Really? BTW, Chomsky doesn't have much good to say about evolutionary psychology.

Next, I found an interview of his about life after COVID-19. Pretty much doom and gloom. Maybe because he's old. I have a theory that we don't live much longer than a hundred because that's about all we can take.

Is it important what people have said about me? Of course. I already told you that "Limelight" used to be my anthem. I have binders full of positive rejections of the books I did not manage to sell. Some of my writer friends actually envied my "wonderful" rejections back then. One read, "I love your words on a page. Now write a story." The problem—I thought I was! Great disadvantage back in those days, living in Jamestown. Hard to find other writers.

And *no*, I don't like people telling me what I am trying to say. Like Humpty Dumpty, I say what I say because I mean what I mean. Of course, there's not a lot to worry about with picture books. But the best part: *Just Like My Dad* was all my grandchildren's favorite book when they were toddlers. And they had no idea at that age that Gramma had written it—before any of them were born. Now that's payment.

I say I want recognition. On the other hand, I'm afraid "they" are going to find out I'm a phony. I actually taught a few classes at our community college. Now that I look back, I was awful. When I was writing, people would ask where I got my ideas. I thought everyone was like me. Ideas came from nowhere and everywhere and would hit me insisting to be written RIGHT NOW—while I was working on something else.

When I opened the store, people then asked, "When are you going to write a book about ice cream? What better subject for children?" But nothing would come. Not one idea. Except for a new jelly or one of the other hundred things I created.

Now that I have finished reading my book about thinkers through the mid-twentieth century, I thought it might be fun to look at thinkers of today. Google says there are no true thinkers of the twenty-first century. What do you think?

I never much liked what I considered to be modern history, the nineteenth/twentieth centuries. Now it seems I can't get enough. I would blame it on the Western philosophy book, but it started before that. How do you decide what to read?

A copy of the letters magazine you started is on its way. Looking forward to seeing it.

Do you remember signing my 1961 yearbook? In it, you marked each of your pictures with a little comment: shy me, coy me, dominant me. One says mature me. But I still want to see the mature-mature you. That is one advantage to texting that I like—the photos you can share. You talk about selfies in one of your posts. I need one.

Have a wedding coming up August first. My middle grandson. His fiancée called this morning and invited me to her dress fitting. I felt honored. Have barely been out of the house over the past four months. I was the one taking the videos when he proposed. We were in Iceland. I thought it terrible that such a romantic moment included a grandmother. But they loved it. And the waterfall behind them was glorious.

I was a pretty good pitcher when I was young. In fact, boys would choose me to be on their team (I was very young), so I still can't forgive World War II society for taking competitive sports away from women in my era. Especially me! My daughter's basketball team was the first SUHS team to win sections. My granddaughter's volleyball team was the first SUHS team to win a state title! The first! And they are female! But I digress....

It seems obvious that pitching is my forte. It also seems apparent that I have little control over my pitches. Then again, I cannot imagine never catching. How grand a day becomes when I've caught a letter in my mailbox (almost as good as a positive rejection—and it seems to take about as long). It's the hitting I avoid. I no longer have any desire to do all those school visits that come with publication, though there was a time I loved them.

So, I still have a fifty-fifty chance of seeing you? Not bad odds. Seems I'm always hoping for something. And usually, it's another letter. I'm addicted.

P.S. Just wondering. How does one feel infinite? Don't think I ever have.

In this letter, he suggested he may be heading "away from letters, that is, with the, um, split vision that they (letters) entail... The split between the person you're writing to, I mean, and whatever it is outside of that person that you want to talk about."

Now I was thoroughly confused. Was he saying he no longer wanted to write letters to me?

He went on. "Maybe I'm just taking my hobby-horse out for a ride." And neatly side-steps all other questions I had thrown his way. But I was feeling better, had a bit more hope.

Then there was this P.S.: "See how much, maybe most of this would fit a blog better than a personal letter?" (Huh?)

Letter 9: July 2020

Beginning to think you are right. Letters are better than books. Of course, they too can bring negative news (Aunt Harriet died, etc.), but usually nothing like warnings about infotech and biotech taking over the world. And soon! That comes from books. And I guess it depends on who is doing the writing. Had never heard of infotech and biotech and I was doing just fine, or so I thought. We grew up in that happy time, right after World War II. So naïve. So ignorant. But isn't that how it should be? Ride the wave until it peters out.

Nazism and Communism are gone. Democracy will soon be too. All were doomed to failure anyway. Let the algorithm rule the world.

Where's the asteroid when we need it? This hypothesis seems more like a slow death by cancer. Am coming close to burying my head in the sand again. Why does it matter in the scheme of things if humanity fades away? Another failed experiment of nature.

Now we come to evolutionary psychology. Again! What about my offspring? My genes must go on! But to where? A world controlled by the internet? By computers? Google, Facebook, Amazon. I love some of them! But I hate them too!

Help! I need something positive to read. Or maybe I should just stop reading. You say literature distances. Why do I feel caught in the middle of something I have no control over?

Letters *are* fun!! There is someone on the other end to catch all your gobbledygook. But the best thing is that, unlike in books, it's only one person. Much less damage done.

But now for some good news. I have finally found an algorithm I understand.

$b \times c \times d$ =ahh

Am I finally getting logic? Know what it means? Biological knowledge multiplied by computing power multiplied by data equals the ability to hack humans. (That's from Yuval Noah Harari.) Cheery thought.

Maybe it's time to give up books again and get back to rug-making. At least that is positive. Something useful and sometimes quite striking—all made from throwaways. I promised myself I would slow down on pitching. Unfortunately, I rarely listen.

Letter 10: July 2020

———— ❖ ————

Google is wrong. There are twenty-first-century thinkers, and Harari is a good one. Are you familiar with him? Some of what he says echoes a bit what you say in your blog. But now I feel embarrassed about everything I have ever written in my letters. How can I believe in souls? In hope? Everything we live is "a fiction"? Religion, patriotism, law. The only truth is that we exist? But I take heart in the fact that science cannot figure out the connection between the brain and mind (consciousness). No one has yet been able to explain what that little spark we call life is. I watched it leave Gina. She was there, then she wasn't. Though I was still holding her body in my arms. This was not the only time I witnessed this. I liked that Harari says something about there being a god of the universe and a god of law, which he calls fiction. But he doesn't call the god of the universe fiction.

I'll shut up now. I probably have everything he said scrambled anyway. All in all, *21 Lessons for the 21st Century* is an excellent read. I hope you are burning my letters.

I am now reading Harari's *Sapiens: A Brief History of Humankind.* He talks about "snail mail," saying people only wrote letters "when they had something important to relate." (Uh-oh). He goes on to claim that both letter and response were "considered carefully." Definitely not me. Might be time to work on my control before I have to forfeit my pitching position.

My copy of the magazine you published all those years arrived in the same mail as your letter. Fun to see it at last. Just skimming for now, but in the comments section readers were discussing whether they share the fact that they are letter writers. It caught my attention. Interesting how reticent most were. I don't get it. I would never feel as uncomfortable as many of them seem to be. That being said, no one on this end knows about our letter exchange. But to me, this is like comparing apples to oranges. I will share eventually, but for now, it is delicious having my secret and wondering how "they" can't know.

Did my kids crave attention? My kids were each fierce competitors in their own right. Each won best athlete of their graduating class, so they each got the recognition they craved. Perhaps that's why they never seemed to feel the need to compete with each other. BTW, Buddha says that's our problem—craving—and once we can overcome this, all is nirvana.

You have a lawyer in the family? Growing up as a daughter of a lawyer in Tuolumne County was a good thing. There were only four practicing in those days. When is the last time you were up this way? Things have changed a lot, yet not.

Do you ever find that you say things in a letter or blog post that you would never say in a social situation? I'm wondering if I could ever write a blog? I've decided I might be able to write one concerning any one of the dozens of things I've done in my life—child-rearing, cooking, crafts—but I don't think I could write what I'm sending to you in a blog. In many ways, I'm playing, but in other ways, I'm quite serious. I want to communicate with one, not a sea of unknowns. Because I know you, but don't "know" you. (My new favorite thought.) In doing this, I am learning about me. And it's about time. We all have our self-images, but how close are we to right?

You say you are "heading away from letters." I couldn't quite get the rest of your meaning, but it seems you want to stop exchanging letters and return to your blog. I would love to follow your blog, but I'm not sure I would ever respond to a post with a comment. And I do not know why. Even what isn't personal is personal to me, I guess.

I know I have said it many times, but if it wasn't for this COVID thing, I probably would never have done this. COVID has forced time to build up in a way I've never experienced. And I am grateful. I have very much enjoyed these past couple months. But I get the feeling you have had enough. I have been told more than once that I can be a bit overwhelming. Sorry.

P.S. I was serious about burning my letters.

Now I am confused. Just noticed your P.S. on the back of the card where you want me to "See how much, maybe most, of this would fit a blog letter better than a personal letter?" To be honest, I'm not sure how it works as either. As a personal letter, I am not sure what you are trying to tell me—as you can probably see from what I have written. (That's why I am leaving everything as is.) As a blog post, it is even more confusing. Maybe a focus on the "split vision" would work. I wasn't sure about "whatever it is outside of that person that you want to talk about" means. When I write a letter, it's about what I want to talk about, what I am thinking at the moment, and I feel it would be no different if I was writing a blog. Though I might focus a bit better knowing there may be a sea of people rather than one. I became even more confused when you went into you and D on the back porch. What were you trying to tell me?

And from a blog perspective, I don't know. Next you jump back to Emily, privacy, your daughter, chimpanzees, and beetles. If you threw this into a blog, I'm not sure anyone would have a clue what you were writing about. I have an idea because it comes from our personal letters. But even so, I'm confused and had no idea how to respond. Might be even more confusing to a blog reader who hadn't the benefit of the back story. Then you come back to "taking your hobby horse out for a ride" and my pen pal is back. Not sure where I belong in all this.

And I have finally figured out how the magazine works. What a fun idea. The publisher was bragging that they have just passed your fifty-one issues and seems quite proud of it. I would have loved working on something like this. I love research. Digging up old letters would have been delicious. I see that the magazine numbers are now in the thirteen thousands. What number did you begin with? That's a lot of letter writers. But going through the category list, I only see a couple that intrigue me enough that I might consider popping off a note. I like the potluck section the most.

That's the thing. I don't think I am writing letters just to be writing letters. I have many writer friends who would write me back –eventually. We all prefer the quick fix of today. Questions resolved in the blink of an eye. But I have enjoyed this back-and-forth—because it is you. I want to know about you. I want you to know about me. And I feel I get both in this exchange. I can get the same thing from your blog, I guess. But that you is more diluted, and I can't ask questions.

Write your blog. Write about those little things that pique your interest. That's where you are best. You have often made me curious enough to pursue something further—and I have enjoyed the journey. Very much.

I had heard nothing from him for weeks, yet there were still things I was finding that I thought might interest him and I wanted to share. One morning I decided, why not? What was there that made me feel I had stay within the confines of back and forth? What would happen if I simply wrote when I wanted to? Hadn't I already set the precedent more than once? Off the letter went.

Letter 11: July 2020

———— ❋ ————

I had thought to send only a few quotes you might enjoy then felt driven to include a few comments. A surprise, I know. Once I said I didn't look for myself in books but often saw myself. We were talking fiction there, but the following covers how I have been feeling about a lot of the garbage I have pitched your way the past few weeks. Dennett says we are not always responsible for what comes from our mouths (fingers too, I'm hoping) so you have not been seeing the real me. (*Riiiiiight.*)

"In response to perceived challenges real or imaginary, we let our boundaries shrink: I didn't do that! That wasn't the real me."

"Yes, the words came out of my mouth, but I refuse to recognize them as my own."

If we were animals, we would have no such problems.

"The sort of consciousness such animals enjoy is dramatically truncated, compared to ours. A bat, for instance, not only can't wonder if it is Friday; it can't even wonder whether it's a bat; there is no role for wondering to play in its cognitive structure.

While a bat, like even the lowly lobster, has a biological self, it has no selfy self to speak of—no Center of Narrative Gravity, or at most a negligible one. No words-on-the-tip-of-its-tongue, but also no regrets, no complex yearnings, no nostalgic reminiscences, no grand schemes, no reflections on what it is like to be a cat, or even on what it is like to be a bat."

—*Consciousness Explained* by Daniel C. Dennett and Paul Weiner

The above has climbed onto the top of the list of my favorite quotes. But as I grow older, I find myself wondering more and more often if it's Friday? So at least I'm not a bat.

Below is exactly how we (the world) got into this mess we are in and why you gave up books for letters (as I see it).

In the ancient past of *homo sapiens*, Members of a band knew each other very intimately and were surrounded throughout their lives by these few friends and relatives. Loneliness and privacy were rare.

Then came communication.

The difference between us and chimpanzees is the mythical glue (fiction?) that binds together a large number of individuals, families, and groups. This glue has made us masters of creation.

The secret was probably the appearance of fiction. A large number of strangers can cooperate successfully by believing in common myths.

The beginning of *them* and *us*?

Yet none of these things exists outside the stories that people invent and tell one another. There are no gods in the universe, no nations, no money, no human rights, no laws, and no justice outside humankind's common imagination.

Now back to our enigma.

In human beings, as we have seen, those practices mainly involve incessant bouts of storytelling and story-checking, some of it factual, some fictional. Children practice this aloud. (Think of Snoopy saying to himself as he sits on his doghouse roof, *Here's the World War I flying ace*. We adults do it more elegantly: silently, tacitly, effortlessly. The philosopher Kendall Walton (1973, 1978) and the psychologist Nicholas Humphrey (1986) have shown from different perspectives the importance of drama, storytelling, and the more fundamental phenomenon of make-believe in providing practice for human beings who are novice self-spinners. (Derived from Daniel C. Dennett and Paul Weiner, *Consciousness Explained*]

I thought this quote was spot-on, too:

"Previously, it took a lot of work to write a letter, address and stamp an envelope, and take it to the mailbox. It took days or weeks, maybe even months, to get a reply. Nowadays, I can dash off an email, send it halfway around the globe, and (if my addressee is online) receive a reply a minute later. I've saved all that trouble and time, but do I live a more relaxed life? Sadly not. Back in the snail-mail era, people usually only wrote letters when they had something important to relate. Rather than writing the

first thing that came into their heads, they considered carefully what they wanted to say and how to phrase it. They expected to receive a similarly considered answer. Most people wrote and received no more than a handful of letters a month and seldom felt compelled to reply immediately. Today, I receive dozens of emails each day, all from people who expect a prompt reply."

—Harari, Sapiens

Not sure about the "considered carefully" part. I know I am half-addicted to the instant gratification of immediacy. But there is still something to be said for anticipation. Besides, everything I have to relate is important, isn't it?

One more thing. As for Dawkins: I am really tired of this science/theology debate. Nothing but a power struggle. And it disappoints me how much time is spent on something that doesn't matter. Haven't we always been taught *show, don't tell*? You put it perfectly. His writing does "kind of slide off the edges."

Letter 12: July 2020

From Dawkins:

> *"I want to begin with the childhood phenomenon of imaginary friend, which I believe has affinities with religious belief."*

Christopher Robin, I presume, did not believe that Piglet and Winnie the Pooh really spoke to him. But was Binker different?

Binker

"Binker—what I call him—is a secret of my own

And Binker is the reason why I never feel alone.

Playing in the nursery, sitting on the stair,

Whatever I am busy at, Binker will be there.

Oh, Daddy is clever, he's a clever sort of man,

And Mummy is the best since the world began,

And Nanny is Nanny, and I call her Nan—

But they can't see Binker."

—A.A. Milne, *Now We Are Six*

More from Dawkins:

"I suspect that the Binker phenomenon of childhood may be a good model for understanding theistic belief in adults. I do not know whether psychologists have studied it from this point of view, but it would be worthwhile research. Companion and confidant, a Binker for life: that is surely one role that God plays—one gap that might be left if God were to go.

A being may exist only in the imagination, yet still seem completely real to the child, and still give real comfort and good advice. Perhaps even better: imaginary friends—and imaginary gods—have the time and patience to devote all their attention to the sufferer. And are much cheaper than psychiatrists or professional counselors."

I came across the above in Richard Dawkins' *The God Delusion* and thought of your daughter. My only issue is that throughout the book he insists that children are only religious because religion is pushed down their throats from birth. Does this not become a chicken-or-egg scenario—if God is no more than a grown-up Binker?

After a long dry spell, here it came. His letter.

"Wow, how neat, those pages you sent on Binker. Now I want to find both of the people, Milne and Dawkins. Many thanks."

"There's no question but that we do love our own most of all. Loving one's neighbors takes a back seat. Way back."

"Christ's injunction to love thy neighbor as thyself becomes all the more pointed, and impossible, when rendered as 'Love thy neighbor as thy kin.' Not likely anytime soon."

Letter 12: August 3, 2020

———— ❖ ————

I am writing this on what would have been my 57th anniversary. And well into *The Moral Animal*. More and more, I feel the need to apologize for my emotional tirade when you pointed out evolutionary psychologists' take on grief. At the time I was not aware of evolutionary psychology per se. Had read many things I now realize were inspired by it, but I was truly ignorant of the origins. I now find myself fascinated.

Seeing how spot on, in my experience, evolutionary psychologists are in their theory of the how and why of human mating choices makes me even more curious about other EP theories. Boy, did Jack and I fit neatly into their niches. Over the past two years, I had begun to realize this on my own, but does this book open my eyes! Remember when I commented on often seeing myself in books, even when not looking? Now I feel someone has been looking over my shoulder, watching, for more than fifty years. A little scary, but what's more disconcerting is how neatly I fit into their box.

As you may know, I had a number of beaus in my youth. Finding "someone" was never a problem for me. I was first attracted to Jack when I was a freshman. He was a senior, and it was the end of the year when he dumped me for the first time. I often wonder if it wasn't for the same reason my previous boyfriend had broken up with me. ("I really, really like you, but a guy needs more, and Bobbi will give it to me.") Not sure it made me smile then, but it sure does now. Anyway, Jack broke up with me just before his graduation and took a classmate named Carol to the all-night party. (Confession: I maneuvered Mike L. into taking me to that party where Jack tried to talk me into letting him take me home. I didn't—which has always made me extremely proud.)

Now to get down to the evolutionary psychology of me as a female of our species.

If I remember right, I asked you out the first time to the Sadie Hawkins dance. Between boyfriends, I was "shopping." Here's what I saw—cute, smart, athletic, and the son of a dentist. Mom was disappointed when I married Jack, a rancher, and not you (but that soon resolved itself and he grieved her early death).

Anyway, as a female sapien, I recognized Jack's potential early on. Women loved him, which made him all-the-more desirable. And he was obsessed with me. And we both wanted children. At that time, I could have cared less for further education. (Well, maybe a little. But it seemed worth the sacrifice, no matter my mother's admonitions that forever was a long time.)

I think I can truthfully say I would change very little of those 57 years. But I will also say that it is a good thing I have always loved a challenge.

There may have been a hint of jealously in our dating years, but he never acted like he owned me—until after we married. Not that I didn't live my life mostly the way I wanted. But it took nearly forty years for me to make him understand that I was not a bit player in his life. I saw myself as his co-star. It was then we actually became best friends. It has been good for me to see that our relationship was far from unusual. I was always ready to blame myself—for everything. And I am not a weak woman. But the way I saw it, I brought nothing to our marriage but me.

He was always the flirt, and to be honest, this pleased me in many ways because I had something others wanted. And he was definitely a better provider than most. (Sound familiar in the EP sense?)

I never cheated on him (my choice), though I felt the need to point out more than once that jealousy isn't flattering—that it often pushes a female to seek out someone who understands her. I would be flabbergasted to learn that he ever cheated on me, no matter his flirtations. (Is this simply ego in me?)

Maybe things simply turned after forty years because by then I was thick, saggy, and my daughters were the ones drawing attention. But I swear, even then, he assumed every male at every conference I ever attended was scheming to get me into bed. Flattering? Not!

Haven't reached the chapters on grief in my evolutionary psychology book yet, but I'm betting I will see myself there too.

Jack and Tricia sitting in front of their ice cream parlor,
Here's the Scoop

Because I had recently mentioned Yuval Harari, his next letter shares a lot of his wondering about things he has read. Was Harari's father somehow connected with the investigation of the happenings at the Olympic games in Munich in 1972? "My imagination ricochets off such personal tangents, prompted by my love for the dramatic," he says.

Letter 13: August 2020

Your comments about Harari's father got me curious. Wikipedia says only that he was a state-employed armaments engineer. No name. Further research uncovered Michael Harari, a Mossad agent, who headed up Operation God of Wrath. Could a state-employed armaments engineer whose job was classified have in real life been a Mossad agent? The mystery grows. And you think your brain is sliding towards doddering? No way.

My sisters were both here for my grandson's wedding a couple weeks ago and sister Pam came up with a project for us—a childhood memoir. She makes books and binds them. Does a fantastic job.

Anyway, she has already finished her part, which seems like more of a description of the house we lived in and of my parents. But it's a great launching pad for my take—if I ever start. This is the part I thought might interest you.

"Tricia had a vivid imagination," she wrote. I think I mentioned earlier that I thought I had some experience with fantasies. Pam says, "Tricia would describe the magical kingdom that was hidden just beyond the cracks in the corner of the wall. There were purple hippos, pink striped zebras, friendly alligators. Oh, yes! Monkeys were swinging on thick vines and there were beautiful castles with every kind of candy swinging from the trees."

I wonder how many siblings share their fantasy friends? I had completely forgotten any particulars, except I knew that my critters could journey from our upstairs bedroom to the bathtub a story below.

While looking for something else, I came across a book called *Imaginary Companions and the Children Who Create Them* by Marjorie Taylor. So I read it (skimmed it, actually). I don't recommend it unless you wonder why your daughter had imaginary friends. Lots of speculation and clinical case studies. Seems that over 60% of children have them at some point for differing reasons. One interesting question was whether animal friends should be included, and in the end, it was decided that they should, so long as it wasn't a favorite teddy bear or something.

Animals that "served as companions" should be considered. Another interesting question was how much parents should be involved. It was decided some participation was positive, but there was a warning: "It may be critical to take a supporting part in this play, rather than attempt to direct activities." Could this have been what upset your daughter? That she misunderstood why you were trying to film her? I'm wondering if your daughter's outrage at you trying to film her "friends" stemmed from her understanding that they were imaginary.

Perhaps she felt you were making fun. Psychologists say that most children realize their "friends" are pretend and that up to two thirds of children have them.

Who are your favorite nonfiction authors? I especially enjoyed *Consciousness Explained* by Dennett, but it was written in the late 1980s. What an eye opener it was to see how far computers have come since he wrote it! So, now I look for books that were written after 2010—unless something really grabs me.

You mentioned *Moral Animal*, so I read it and couldn't help but wonder when you read it. Some of your blog posts sound as though you may have been reading it at the time you were writing. (Speaking of the blog, I see no activity, and I've been watching.) Anyway, reading the book got me thinking about rage. Your rage at the survivor of your brother's accident, mine at really stupid things. Most things eventually slide off my back, but there are two things that make my blood boil. One is that no matter how far in advance I order my prescriptions, they are never ready when I go to pick them up. "Computer problems" is always the reason. But this is nothing compared to how angry it makes me when people pass in the merge lane. Where are they going? Why are they so much more important than the rest of us? Wright says in his *Moral Animal*, "The basic paradox here—the intellectual groundlessness of blame, and the practical need for it—is something few people seem eager to acknowledge." But why do we "need" blame? Life is so much easier without it. I tell myself it does not matter every time I stop at the light. But there have been times I have actually considered pulling in front of someone—thus committing a like "sin." What is wrong with me? Then I read Robert Sapolosky's *Behave: The Biology of Humans at their Best and Worst.* I bet you would love it—academic, long, but such writing, with humor lubricating all the right places. A small example might entice you:

"Here are two examples of just how strange and unique humans can be when they go about harming one another and caring for one another. The first example involves, well, my wife. So, we're in the minivan, our kids in the back, my wife driving. And this complete jerk cuts us off, almost causing an accident, and in a way that makes it clear that it wasn't distractedness on his part, just sheer selfishness. My wife honks at him, and he flips us off. We're livid, incensed. Asshole-where's-the-cops-when-you-need-them, etc. And suddenly my wife announces that we're going to follow him, make him a little nervous. I'm still furious, but this doesn't strike me as the most prudent thing in the world. Nonetheless, my wife starts trailing him, right on his rear. After a few minutes, the guy's driving evasively, but my wife's on him. Finally, both cars stop at a red light, one that we know is a long one. Another car is stopped in front of the villain. He's not going anywhere. Suddenly my wife grabs something from the front seat divider, opens her door, and says, 'Now he's going to be sorry.' I rouse myself feebly—'Uh, hon, do you really think this is such a goo—' But she's out of the car, starts pounding on his window, I hurry over just in time to hear my wife say, 'If you could do something that mean to another person, you probably need this,' in a venomous voice. She then flings something in the window. She returns to the car triumphant, just glorious.

'What did you throw in there?' She's not talking yet. The light turns green, there's no one behind us, and we just sit there. The thug's car starts to blink a very sensible turn indicator, makes a slow turn, and heads down a side street in the dark at, like, five miles an hour. If it's possible for a car to look ashamed, this car is doing it. 'Honey, what did you throw in there, tell me?' She allows herself a small, malicious grin. 'A grape lollipop.' I was awed by her savage passive-aggressiveness—'You're such a mean, awful human that something must have gone really wrong in your childhood, and maybe this lollipop will help correct that just a little.' That guy was going to think twice before screwing with us again. I swelled with pride."

How could he know me when he doesn't even know me? I've decided Wright must be right. There are reasons behind how we are "programmed."

71

In his next letter, he remembered that he had read Sapolsky and shares that the reason he remembered was, "I thought at the time how lucky his wife was that she didn't get shot by the angry motorist."

He then turned to memoir, since I had shared with him the project my sisters and I were tackling. "Mary Karr in *The Art of Memoir* talks about the great popularity of the memoir in recent years. From those I've read, the dramatic flourishes in this medium." He wondered, "Did her name come up for you and your sisters in your own memoir project?"

I especially loved these musings, knowing how he loves drama: "So, if Hans Gosling is right (along with his two co-authors), our current appetite for memoirs, and all the drama they usually have, might not be healthy. Maybe it's the fat and sugar and all those carbs we love so well."

In her introduction to *The Art of Memoir,* Mary Karr explains that she is attempting to share with an author a way to discover the story that only they can tell. This seems to hit a nerve: "The letter-preaching rebel in me says, Nope, takes two to make a story, we are not atoms, singular creatures. A story always has more than one protagonist, even if the other one or two or two million, is the listener."

Here again, I have to step back and say, huh?

Letter 14: August 2020

———— ✹ ————

Decided to finish *Imaginary Companions and the Children Who Create Them* by Marjorie Taylor. As I mentioned earlier, I don't recommend it unless you are wondering why your daughter had her imaginary friends. One thing I found interesting is that she claims that "children from families of every size create imaginary companions, (though) firstborn and only children are more likely to do so."

Another thing buzzing in my head is "when we count on strangers to be our witness." Maybe writers need strangers so they can write. Family and friends know you too well—or so they think. Been playing with an idea.

As you can see by my earlier rantings—one minute I feel doomed, the next my heart sings. Been feeding book suggestions to some of my grandsons. Three of them read *Sapiens*. Didn't like the end much, so I pointed them toward Harari's *Humankind*. They need barrels of hope for what their generation is going to face. But hope is there! Just finished *The Green New Deal* by Jeremy Rifkin. We humans can fix our problems—and in time. If I can only stop our damn cows from burping. Oh, the guilt. But I will tell you one thing: When I began this quest, at the beginning of this COVID lockdown, my outlook was pretty grim. Basically, I believed humankind would simply go extinct, and soon. Nothing I can do, so why should I care? My time here grows shorter and shorter, it won't affect me. Serves us right! Even though it ate my guts to think of what my young ones were going to have to face.

Now—and I give credit to my quest—things I've read on your blog, things I've read in your letters, I am loading my toilet paper over the top once more. I am once again a cheerleader, pushing my grandchildren toward hope. Did you know that if our temperatures rise a teeny bit more we humans are doomed? But we can do it. We can overcome. Am I sounding like a zealot? I just know that I am in a better place at this moment (hope-wise) than I was at the beginning of COVID.

As for marriage, if our times are any indication, I wouldn't recommend it as the "best witness to our lives." Looking back through history, how many times has marriage been the "best" witness? There is a huge difference between marriage (a legal binding) and the joining of two souls.

Oops, I forgot. There's no such thing as soul.

Finished *The Lions Club* this morning. Karr is a fabulous writer. But could she really have remembered such detail, being 7 or 8? Her descriptions are amazing, and I can't help but wonder how she does it. But barely halfway through the book, I wanted it over. Not like me. The book is dark. Depressing. And so funny at times. But mostly depressing. One thing that rose to the top is her agnostic struggle.

Then the sun shines again—unless you look outside where smoke from all our fires doesn't even let us see the sun.(My daughter Jodi was evacuated for three days.) Now I want to shout *hallelujah* as I read my latest book *Humankind: A Hopeful Story* by Rutger Bergman. He had been raised with a strict faith but what he was learning made him realize that the notion of evolution was not such a downer anymore. "Maybe there is no creator, no cosmic plan. Maybe our existence is just a fluke after millions of years of blind fumbling. But at least we are not alone. We have each other." I nearly broke into tears.

Then I remember the times in your blog you mention how important other people are to you. How important society is to you. Now I can see why. Sort of. Bergman says, "But Geniuses have a problem. They're not all that social. On average, the Genius who invents the fishing rod has only one friend they can teach to fish. The Copycats, on the other hand, have on average ten friends, making them ten times as social." Because it doesn't take a Genius to design a fishing rod, the word Designer needs to be substituted for Genius in my opinion. Only about 1% of us are creators; Copycats learn to use our stuff and pass this knowledge on. This, pure and simple, has filled in many gaps for me. I have always been a designer. A Genius? Hardly. And some of us design much more important things than others. Many of us designers (writers, crafters, artists, engineers) cling to the very bottom rung, but we still "design."

This morning, I turned on Cohen. *Anthem* brought back the light and a "cold and lonely hallelujah" warms my heart. His words and my soul will always be whatever I want them to be.

And that's when I believe we are blessed to be homo sapiens. Because we can think.

Letter 15: September 2020

———— ❀ ————

You say in a recent letter that your imagination ricochets off such personal tangents as the possibility of Yuval Harari being the son of the man of the in charge of police reprisals against the Palestinian terrorists who murdered Israeli athletes in the 1972 Munich Olympics. My imagination stirs too, but my bout with familial history seems to be poking at a personal smoky memory insisting that it be explored further. Over the years, I have done quite a bit on our family genealogy. I had **no** idea until I got into this that three sides of my tree stretched back to pre-Revolutionary War times. Along the way, I discovered that my mother's side included a number of slave owners (which still embarrasses me, as though our generation was in some way responsible). Anyway, last year, I watched the new release of *Roots*. Early in the movie, they called Kunta's owner by name. My ears perked up. I was sure it was the same name as one of my early ancestors—and he was a nasty man in the movie. Have I followed up? No. And I'm not sure why. But at the moment it feels as though I will be moving this up on my to-do list. At the same time, maybe I'll follow up on this: I did some work on Jack's family tree too, and when I got back into the Carolinas, I ran across what I thought were familiar names. Could we have shared ancestors? Fun. But I haven't followed up there either. And it would be so easy. Typical me, full-bore or back turned.

Also been pondering a them versus us scenario. My cousin was here from Texas last week. I invited them for dinner while they were here, since because of COVID, all restaurants are takeout only. Pam came too. Not so good at small talk any-more, so I brought up some of the interesting stuff I'd been reading. And, of course, it had to be Darwinism. I'd forgotten how far-right Christian she had become until I noticed the look on their faces at something I'd said. A few days later, I posted a picture on Facebook of the hands of my two-month-old great-granddaughter, her mother, her grandmother, and her great-grandmother, all in a row.

My comment: "Evolution in progress." My cousin responded: "Evolution or the reality of life's physiological journey?" Them versus us, and I was the *them*. But why? Then again, is my wonder that all we see has evolved from a couple of elements who found a way to spark life much different from her belief that it was not two elements but a single being responsible for creation? Both are mysterious and impressive. My way of thinking took billions of years to do what God accomplished in six days. But no matter how hard I have tried over the years, it's the "others" mentioned in Genesis that keep me wonder-ing.

Tricia's Magnificent 7

Letter 16: September 2020

———— ❁ ————

You have seen none of what follows. Well, maybe you have, as I'm sure some of these thoughts had to have influenced parts of what I have written in the past months. But most of this comes from my thoughts on things you wrote in your blog. Looks like I was already writing to you before I even found you.

You are right that self-definition is impossible. What comes to mind is all those who obviously cannot see themselves (or even imagine) how others see them. Trump comes to mind. Me also.

- About scapegoats and selfies: I definitely need scapegoats. Never my fault, or is it? Never take selfies, so that isn't the solution. I try walking in other's moccasins, but so often they simply don't fit right, so can I really understand where "they" are coming from?

- What I truly do not understand is how anyone can get so far into self that they cannot look around. We need to simply look around to see how so many others are going through so much worse than we. Does this help? I don't know. But we are definitely not alone.

- One reason for distance (besides COVID): The further we remain from other humans, the less polluted we are by the world we humans have created. I have always believed that if we did the best job we could in everything we do—raising children, etc.—this, like ripples, would radiate outward, improving whatever it touched. Now I wonder if this is not simply another of my theories that falls through the cracks.

Few individuals can be blamed for what has come to be. It takes an accumulation of us. And when we congregate, we seem to lose our "cerebration." Where are the convictions we once held so dear? Is it because we have learned that we have to make deals? Give them what they want in exchange for what we want? The thirst for power plants its roots. An addiction older than any drug? Does any of it truly make one feel better?

I hate when I am not producing. Then I wonder, producing for what? Maybe quiet is good for a time. Be gone my guilt!

Can there ever be a world shaped by reading and writing? How many of our millions read? Barely a pinch of those most in need of that meant for them. Then again, writing obviously does its shaping.

In your blog, you wrote, "One grieves, I believe, not from a feeling of separation but from the opposite. A part of oneself has died, and that is unbearable." How can one not celebrate that the departed was part of their life, no matter how short the time? Human life is finite. Always will be. None of us is forever. Why can we not appreciate and absorb those who have touched us—if only fleetingly—if for no more than to enrich our soul? They lived for a time, therefore they live in our memory, in our hearts.

- Autism and literacy: I see in this you are contradicting your-self. In your words (world), there always need to be two. But for me, wordless music touches my soul, allowing me to soar alone. Then again, someone did write that music.

- I ramble because of all the interesting things your comments stir up in my mind.

- If interaction (giver/receiver) is so important, are you not cheating when you write a blog? For all you know, you may be totally alone—if no one comments.

- Obscenity: What is our obscenity is the new generation's norm. After all, language, like life, is ever-evolving.

- There is a right—what's right for you. But can't we be satis-fied with keeping our personal right to ourselves, without feeling the need to push it on others? Then again, I wonder how our world would look if no one had ever done so?

- A writer writes to play with their thoughts—to ground these thoughts and wondering.

- Sure, Thoreau distanced himself from civilization. Still, his thoughts broke free to enlighten us with such insights as, "There is no remedy for love but to love more."

- Writing is one person's opinion, one person's quest. The reader only "hears" what speaks to them.

- I love the thought of living "with one's own self-contradictions." The best part of being human, the continuous quest for the real you.

- *"Every generation has the obligation to free men's minds for a look at a new world...to look out from a higher plateau than the last generation."* This is a quote by Ellison Onezuka, found on American passports. Unfortunately, as we well know, the number of those who look out seems to shrink with each generation. Or is that simply age grumping?

- When I was young, I imagined my words, my thoughts, might make a difference. Get real! But sometimes touching only one person can make a difference. Is this enough?

- Literacy and monotheism: Whether or not you believe in a God, how can you not simply celebrate and give thanks for the greatest gift you will ever receive? Life! A magical thing. And it can be shaped.

- I believe words are the magic from which so many "things" can be made.

- Conclusions seem to be ever-changing. A good thing.

- Yes, many of us covet the spotlight. You crave the satisfaction of someone embracing your words, your thoughts. One of my favorite songs goes, "Limelight shining on me, telling the world who I am" by Alan Parsons Project.

- You are so wrong that men keep score more than women. Many of us can't help but compete, even against ourselves. Why?

- I've never "made" much money, no matter what I tackled. But I always understood that money was the measure of success. Then, one day, I overheard two women discussing, with wonder and admiration, things I had created. I realized this was the only payment I craved. Money was simply frosting on the cake. But (this too I realized) I never needed money to support my family, to support anything other than creating more. I was spoiled. Does this make a difference? Is this fair?

- How many times have I thought to write my memoirs, my interpretation of how best to face this journey we call life? I have done and experienced so much and appreciated every minute of my journey—both good and bad—for it has led here. A good place to be. Maybe this is why I enjoy being alone. I want no corruption, no pollution, of this feeling I have achieved. It can hit from anywhere, most times when unexpected.

- Throw ideas my way, but never try to push them on me. I do hear and sometimes may even embrace them—those that touch something within me.

- Back to obscenities. We look for our best (our easiest) descriptives. Shit has always been that for me (much to my parents' irritation.) But I ask you, is there any better, more universal, description?

- I know about myself—or what I think is myself—and that is why I want to know about you. In knowing—whether it be you, a grandchild, a friend—I learn more about myself.

- I hide so much of myself from those I love. Why? Because I am bent on burying my faults? I was 75 years old before I shared with my children that I was not a virgin when I married. Telling.

- "Sunrise, sunset, sunrise, sunset, swiftly fly the years. One season following another, laden with happiness and tears." Words to live by from Fiddler on the Roof. Words to keep in mind when all else seems lost. How can we possibly appreciate the view from the top if we have never experienced the blackness at the bottom?

- Back to that virginity thing. Why did I think of losing it as a fault? Sex is the driving force of nature—the drive to communicate in every way. Sometimes for love. Sometimes solely for recreation. But I see it as a good thing that my grandchildren have not felt such restrictions. It is never good to marry someone simply because you slept with them. Sex should always be a sidebar. The frosting on the cake. I love mixing metaphors.

- Now that I think about it, my life has been pregnant with guilt. At seven, I headed a Robin Hood gang, which included Pam, who was five, and a neighbor, Mimi, who was two years older than me. Where did I get such a connection to Robin Hood at this young age? Books? Movies? I have no idea. But how I admired him! So, we stole from "the rich" (our parents)—but I don't remember ever giving to the poor. Instead,

I took some of the money, walked over a mile to the middle dime store, and bought a bow with arrows. Didn't concern me a bit that the arrows were tipped with rubber suction cups. I would remove the suctions and sharpen the tips in a pencil sharpener, so I could hunt food for my "merry men." Perhaps it was the two $20 bills Mimi took from her father's wallet (that was a lot of money back in those days). All we could find in my father's stash was a bit of change. One morning, I pilfered a few coins and gave them to Pam to keep in her shoe. To this day, I have no idea why I didn't simply keep them in mine? Living out the Robin Hood code in kindergarten, Pam began passing coins around to her classmates. That afternoon, who shows up at our hideout? Our mom and Mimi's mom. It was over. And as my mom strongly pointed out, it was a sin! My first Communion was coming up that summer. How could I admit to such a thing? Surely, I would be damned forever. But did that stop me? Sin is a challenge, after all.

- It takes two to make a thought? I immediately agreed with this until I began pondering. What came first, the chicken or the egg? If a tree falls in the forest...? All that truly matters are the words and how they land on who hears them.

- Heard on the way to the bank on the station I listen to most: "On Broadway," a song about John Wilkes Booth in which the singer comments about Lincoln getting "mixed reviews" before Booth's actions. Got me wondering... just how important is timing? I have marveled at how things have lined up at the right time in the right place in my life. Why does this happen to some, yet not to others? Some lose several spouses, others total several cars. I never stop remembering the family losing their fifth child to the same genetic disorder at UC Med Center when we were losing Gina.

- I've tried journaling from time to time over the years. Something I never stuck with, no matter how much I claim to prefer being alone with my thoughts. But now when I "see" you while I am writing, everything seems to flow. Maybe you are right about needing two: the pitcher and the catcher. It's sometimes nice picturing you on the receiving end. Thank you for your blog. Finding it is one more instance of perfect timing.

- It is not the decline of males, it's putting them in their place. Yes, females have had their crosses to bear, but can this incessant complaining bang things into their rightful place? Maybe. Mention does trigger thought. But evolution takes time, including social evolution. I remember wondering in the sixties how soon civil rights would take their rightful place. In my mind, I thought it would probably take about another hundred years. Today we find ourselves more than halfway there. Have things changed? Some. I remember when you rarely saw a Black person on television, then came Bill Cosby in I Spy. How we loved him! How unfair in some ways that he set civil rights progress back a few steps because of his antics. Lately I notice most families we see on commercials are mixed-race. And "just like us." But who is us?

Humans come at things from so many directions. Won't there always be an us versus them? Isn't that what makes us human—an ever-changing *them*? I think I have known this for a long time. I recently ran across this note I wrote to myself on the back of an envelope: "We humans come in many different varieties, thus we ball up with others like us to build our comfort zone." This has me feeling odd-man-out, but I do it to myself.

There are few places I *want* to belong. Religion doesn't work for me. Organizations, clubs, boards don't work for me (yet I recognize how much we need them). Why? Family has always been my anchor, and now I'm wondering if I'm not pulling away here, too? All because of a group text message to my family that I truly believed was well thought out. I had heard, and read about, how many families have been disrupted by COVID, not necessarily from deaths, but from disagreement over the efficacy of vaccines. Have none of them ever heard Bjorn Lomborg's contention that "vaccines now save more lives **each year** than would have been spared had we had world peace for the *entire twentieth century*"? Sure, he's controversial, but it's something to at least think about. A concept I would love to believe. But where's the proof? Show me, I want to believe.

In this I could agree with my grandchildren but not with their arguments, their reasons for not getting vaccinated as they now stand. From what I hear, this family division is strongest between grandparent and grandchild. Would never happen to me, I fantasized. Wrong! Wrong! and again wrong. And I feel like the bad guy. I probably am the bad guy.

I cannot make myself roll over and pretend the logic of the un-vaccinated is right. I attended a wedding that in my gut didn't feel right. I accepted my anti-vaccine grandchildren into my house. Though I was uncomfortable, I kept my mouth shut. And now I feel like I am paying for it. Why? This question has been banging around in my head for the past five days. Here is what I have come up with: I am not afraid of the virus. In fact, part of me wonders if we shouldn't have let it run its course? The population would have been cut way back. Humankind might have been given a bit of a breather before extinction. Then again, what else might this particular unchallenged virus have stirred up? Now I'm wondering if I don't simply add too much drama to everything? Because I am a writer?

What I have discovered is that I am judgmental. Of everyone. How right is this for someone who believes that every adult has the right to build their own right? How can I make myself remember that our right is only right for us? I have always claimed, always believed, that family is my focus. But is it? I want to do what I want to do when I want to do it. Not always possible with family. So, we make concessions and assure ourselves that it is worth it—which it is. Mostly.

I know I am an idiot. I've lived with me for well over 75 years. I do care what is happening. But it is what it is. That was Jack's mantra when his life was disintegrating. Yet I do not, will not, back down.

This morning I was watching the hummingbirds beating the shit out of each other at their feeder over nothing. Their feeder is always full. I tell myself, *You are doing the same thing.* But can I stop? Will I stop? For some reason, that got me thinking about Queen Elizabeth (hers is definitely a life I do not envy). She has spent her entire life sacrificing her rights for what she believed was the good of the country, the good of her family. Can there be a better example that sometimes it's time for tradition to change?

Then, there is Tevye in *Fiddler on the Roof* telling us why he does what he does in one word: tradition. In truth, I wonder who this tradition benefits? Would it not make more sense to bend with the winds of time? This thought appeals to me much more than the atmosphere I envision if we do all gather in one enclosed space.

Maybe I simply miss my soulmate. So, few and far between.

- Yes, we are polluting (poisoning) our mother—Earth—with our humanness. But she will have the last laugh, rebuilding herself when we are gone.

- My older cat Edo makes me think of you. My younger cat Silky is me. She teases and teases him unmercifully. It drives him crazy. He used to ask to go outside when he had had enough. But now, no matter how irritated he grows, he hangs in there. In fact, I think he enjoys it, even if only a bit.

- You talk about when you and D first got together. You are not alone in remembering those first stirrings of a new relationship, a new marriage. But every relationship wears and changes in so many ways, as wind and water transform rock into new and beautiful shapes, into soil. But it is up to us to recognize the new, never losing track that some of our best journeys begin with a detour, something we did not foresee.

- Again, I see it another way. Your interpretation of your words should have little to do with "the one you are with." It is their role to take from your words what they need (keeping in mind that few of us require the same exact thing)?

- It seems power comes from how the reader uses your words. I feel driven to write. But what kind of writing? I stand at a crossroads. Do I want to write for publication, or simply to hear myself think? I blame it on the pandemic. I am so not alone, so why am I yearning? And for what? I think I have solved my drive to write and not worry about what I am doing to you. I will write to you and not send. One minute I feel you want to hear from me and the next I feel you want me to stop writing completely. For awhile I wrote nearly three letters to your one, simply because I had things I wanted to say and didn't want to wait. Have never been especially patient, but I am learning how to have my cake and eat it too.

- Here is my latest decision. From now on I will simply jot down my musings, mostly triggered by your blog. And you will no longer have to deal with a lot of what I am thinking. When I write, it's mainly for me anyway, to release some of what builds in my head. (After all, how much room is up there?) On the other hand, I enjoy imagining someone, usually a single someone, reading what I write and wanting to respond. A connection. Why? Why, when like Thoreau, I prefer being alone with my thoughts? (Or so I believe.) Where

91

everything stays as I imagine before anyone else can intrude with their thoughts and tell me what I really mean?

- Why do I write? I write for the joy of building my own something with the same words accessible to all. Why do I not write? It's not because I no longer believe I have the time to write. I have nothing but time. Am I afraid?

- The most important thing we all need to keep in mind is that no matter who is writing—Thoreau, Dostoyevsky, Elizabeth Wayland Barber—the sentiments are from one person's point of view. What they write is one person's interpretation, one person's imagination, one person's accumulation of thoughts in whatever order the writer deems right. I've always believed that much is written simply for a paycheck. It's that from the gut that I look for. When a writer cares about something, it always comes across. Powerfully!

- Isn't that why we all write? To answer a question. Our question. So often dealing with rejection and hurt. Thoreau is certainly not alone. Leave the poor aesthetics alone, there are so few of them. And they are often our thinkers.

- Are you really going to care when you are dead? Why sweat the small stuff? The dead have left. And the use of the word *eclipse* by Emily Dickenson is simply a synonym for death. It feels nothing but right when using the Merriam Webster second definition: a falling into obscurity or decline. What better definition of our passing? Why have you never written a book? Why do you not critique them? You have what it takes, including your education. Some simply listen. Others open their mouths and a dam breaks—me! Damn dam! I try to

imagine you as a "sometimes sissy" and I laugh. And laugh
And laugh.

In September I get the teensiest of peeks into his daily life and wondered if he is finally becoming comfortable with wondering when and from where I will hit again.

Letter 17: September 2020

What a fun letter. Finally, a peek into your daily life. We are so similar. I love to win! I love to think. And read. Does that make me bookish? But there is one area I have you beat by a mile. I am a hundred times more irrational. I heard this last night in a program I was watching: "It's never the one you haven't met, only the one you can't forget." That struck a gong. OMG, that's me. What am I doing? So, now I hope you can bear with me as I pursue this thought. I looked for you for the fun of it and because I heard that you and D were a thing of the past. Then, I discovered that you and D are not entirely over, or are you? But once I had heard from you, I had no desire to let go.

What was I doing? That's why I asked, and D said to tell me "we are best friends." So, there was still room for me, I rationalized. Not really believing it for a minute. But what is your relationship? I have no idea how often you see one another. I know you talk on the phone. Often? How can you be together yet live nearly 1400 miles apart? You speak often of your love for her. *Back off, back off,* I tell myself. What am I looking for?

Someone who likes to think. Someone who likes books. Someone who enjoys communicating about both. And, I'll admit, I like that you are male. The thought of going out and looking for "you" when I already have "you" makes no sense. Besides, where would I look? Bar? Casino, church? Internet? No thank you! I'm not looking for a husband. But I will admit that I might be looking for that comfortable relationship of an old married couple. Here is where the rational you tells me to get lost.

We got back from my sister Tina's in Georgia on Friday. Great trip. Finished our childhood memoirs. Now, Pam has to put everything together. Best flight I've had in years. No one sitting next to me. Airports uncrowded. Everyone wearing masks—except for the jerk sitting in front of me. He refused to put on his mask even when threatened that officials would be waiting for him at the gate. They weren't

What else do we have in common? "Wonky" hearts. Mine has not been behaving since July. Some they catch on my remote, but they still have no idea, so I had a monitor awaiting my arrival home. Will wear for two weeks to see if they can determine what is going on this time. Might be that a Meals on Wheels volunteer like you will soon be bringing me my meals. Not! I am still functional—that's why I chose to go to Tina's now—but very slowed down. I hate it!

Been thinking about all those choices we "will do anything for" according to Wright. In my opinion, respect will always rank number one. Isn't respect what we use to measure our own self-worth? And if we don't like ourselves, who else will?

Love, sex, food... some of us seem more addicted than others. Kids—more than important to some, barely considered by others. This one might require more thinking: aren't we wanted if we are needed? Or needed if we are wanted?

As for winning, this I understand. The good thing I've discovered is that I hate losing more than I love winning. This is what stopped my buying chances when I was playing Wheel of Fortune after Jack died. I was becoming one of those, though I can't quite swallow that a woman spent $400,000 on video slots. Don't they have to use a credit card? Aren't there limits? I do enjoy playing slots from time to time, but I limit myself. Rarely win, so rarely go to the casino. We now have two casinos in the county and more than a few among us are horribly addicted. Mostly I go to Reno a couple times a year to meet my widow friend Louise who loves slots and wins! I spend a lot of time in our room knitting or reading—that tells how well I do.

Loved your admission that you play a card game every morning, that you cheer for yourself and play till you win. I can almost hear the chant you admit to: "Gotta win. Gotta. Gotta," and hear your screams of victory. Even if it's 'only' solitaire you play, do I relate!!! There was a time I played Spider Solitaire for hours to keep my mind from thinking. Now I play Candy Crush—only the free games—every morning. It's become my measure for how my day is going to go. The problem is, playing only free games, it sometimes takes days to win a game. I will not buy a life or a booster. If only I had this much control over the rest of my life. In Candy Crush, we play in leagues with other players and one of my team gets on my nerves because her (Nora's) profile picture is of Christ. This just doesn't seem right, and I hate when she beats me. I still have issues, don't I?

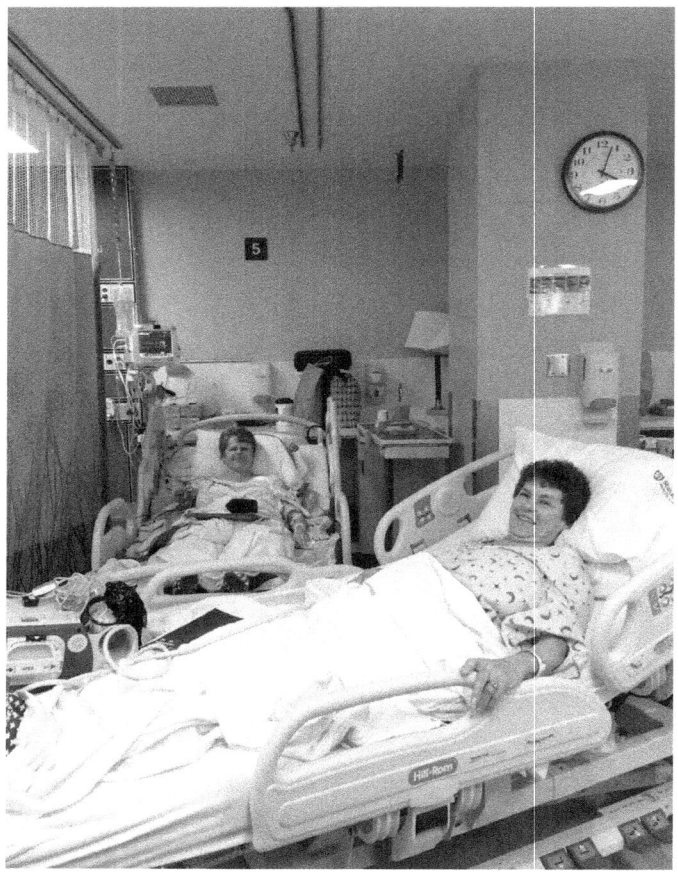

Tricia and sister Tina sharing a moment at Stanford. Tina, recently diagnosed and getting her first defibrillator. Tricia, for one of her many overhauls.

"Books blab at the whole wide world, and all the stars in the sky. A letter talks only to me."

"Call it a joy of old age, maybe, no longer needing other people to tell me who I am."

I appreciate how we seem to be on the same page in all but the difference between letter writing and book writing.

Letter 18 : October 2020

— ❊ —

That's exactly why books are so good. "They blab to the whole wide world and all the stars in the sky." The best ones offer learning and something to think about. A letter talks only to you. But is it about you? Maybe sometimes. Usually, it's simply whatever the writer is thinking at the time. Letters are about the writer, just as books are about the writer.

Of late, I have enjoyed 'talking' to you more than anyone else. It's like I'm peeling off the layers to understand more about me. It made me smile that you needed old age to recognize who you are. I have always known who (what) I am. Someone out of step , someone ever-evolving, someone who talks too much while finding it difficult to communicate, and someone who appreciates the wonder of the entire world, no matter.

Your quote of Emerson that he does not easily forgive the "dullness of perception that talks to every man alike" especially set me off. How self-centered to feel that someone who does not "know" you does not have the right to try to feel his way along to knowing you? And why are "you" more important than he? Don't we all find ourselves feeling our way along at times? Doesn't the speaker have a right to "be known" too? And, no, books do not say the same thing to every person. The words might be the same, but interpretation is very personal.

I appreciate (and love!) how some can take the same words available to everyone and build a wondrous world where I can escape to. Admittedly, there are few who can pull this off, but they are out there. How satisfying when everything lines up just right—mood, need, everything.

I want to know. I want to learn. I want to understand. But it really doesn't matter to me if I ever get there. It's the journey I love. Keep the books coming. (Not that I ever remember a word for more than five minutes!)

But you are right. Letters *are* important! I felt it when I got that postcard. You said, "My words are running fewer and farther between these days. This may be temporary." And I thought I would never get another word from you. You (a male friend) are the only thing missing from my nearly perfect life. I like your words on a page.

Letter 19: November 2020

— ❖ —

8:00. *What a glorious morning!* Can't tell you how many games I've won—and I've beat Nora nearly every time! What a perfect day must be in store for me. But no one is near to hear my hallelujah.

10:00. Today is going to be better than glorious, I'm thinking. Four times in the past few weeks we've been promised rain and have barely gotten a spit. Plants are drying up because I am too lazy to water. Then in the past thirty minutes, clouds have come rolling in and a south wind is more than blustering. John says they are predicting more than in inch tonight. YIP-PEE!!!

Here's what I have been wondering. If I talk to you while I am working, what does that mean? I find myself arguing against quite a few of your claims. And I wonder what you do every day with no internet, TV, newspaper, or radio? Can you listen to music? Watch DVDs? I'm fine with little outside communication. Haven't watched or read local news for years. Not that I think that's a great attitude. But during these election finals, I've been tuning into PBS news in the evening and thereby discovered two Japanese news programs, as well as two BBC, and I'm hooked. At least for a while. The Japanese commentators have no accents. Wow!

Maybe I told you: I canceled Thanksgiving. Doing a drive-thru Sort of fun. Middle daughter says we could do a virtual feast through Google. Up to her to set that up, if she wants. But do we really need to watch each other chewing? She has been doing virtual teaching for the past several months. Not the best method for a PE teacher.

One of the things I was discussing with you while I was doing my chores is that your sister is right—family is important. It's not all about you. Remember you are not going to be here forever. They simply want contact while you are. I don't think I ever met either of your sisters.

I'm now thinking how lucky you are not to have a media connection. Things are scary right now, especially when you learn that Germany was a democracy shortly before Hitler's rise to power. And especially how our president is acting at the moment.

December was when I began really screwing things up. He didn't mind the first package I sent. It was the second that he said was still sitting on his counter and had no desire to open. To be honest, I doubt it was my packages so much as a couple things from our past that I shared that began to spiral our communication downward, one was a picture of me wearing his athlete sweater, the other was something he had written in my yearbook. Too much. I should have known better. And I was sorry.

Letter 20: December 2020

---❊---

You really know how to hurt a girl. Selective amnesia? Maybe. But I sent this ancient Christmas picture because I am wearing your sweater, something I did proudly for the entire school year. I really don't remember much about our time together, but what I do remember is that I was proud to be your girlfriend. There was so much I admired and loved about you, plus a few things I didn't understand. And then there is this delicious, warm, and caring ego booster you wrote in my yearbook. I send it hoping to remind you of another time, to show that you once truly cared. Sadly, it seems time brought with it selective amnesia. I sent it because I wanted so much for you to know that there truly was a time. This is the last thing I will ever embarrass you with. Intentionally anyway. I promise!

Do I gloat when I beat Nora? You bet I do! And the very best thing: One day I was playing along the path as I continued winning game after game. More than usual. While negotiating a curve in the path, what do I see to my right? A picture of Christ. A few games later, I passed it. Have never seen Nora again.

Letter 21: January 2021

---※---

Your scolding is well-taken. Of course, you are right: "our past time together is just that, closed." But does this mean our present connection should be closed too? Mostly both of us seem to enjoy our discussions.

I am sorry that my packages overwhelmed you. I promise I will send no more—unless we are still corresponding next Christmas, and I am still making things. It gives me great pleasure to share things I make with friends this time of year. You were not the only one I sent gifts to. But if you don't like my jelly, that's fine. I guarantee the honey is delicious. It comes from people who have kept bees on our ranch for more than fifty years. And the second package results simply from my warped sense of humor. I had no idea, and I had recently promised to try to no longer do anything to cause you stress. Unfortunately, I seem to have a difficult time with closure. Every experience that has touched me, that has contributed to who I am, stays, making me who I am. Maybe not consciously until some random event opens that file. Though to be fair,

I'm sure there are zillions of happenings buried deep under all the other happenings, so I am guessing that is what you mean.

With that said, I am open to "keep on going." I enjoy how you think about things, as I often mention. And I do love to write.

You are right. I am not religious in the accepted sense. Yet religion is what drives my life. I believe. I believe in whatever it is—whatever it takes—to drive this thing we call the universe. This thing we call life with all its ups and downs amazes me at every turn. Yet at the same time, I feel apologetic. Guilty. Why have I been so blessed? Yes, I have hurt. But nothing like most. And with each hurt, I look for the good, thereby increasing my wonder.

As for family and religion being at odds, not sure I can buy into that. I see religion arising from unanswered questions. Maybe in the beginning, it came from nothing more than what I feel—awe. But soon they had to know. Who was behind all this? And, of course, this is something I doubt we can ever know, thus was born faith, which then led to science, the need to know. But is science really much different? Many scientists have similar faith issues—with more testing, we can know everything. I hope not! I wonder if I don't simply worship the mystery? Is this why I hated when the church turned the altar toward the congregation, no longer reaching out to the unknown?

"Something more in life than family." Family is what life is about. Whether you are a fly, that peacock you once talked about, or us. Procreation. That's the only reason life is part of the universe. Our job is simple: to keep our kind going. Humans are the only life form to believe there is something more to it. To me, it makes no difference. If I die tomorrow and there is nothing more, oh well. If life goes on, another adventure. Maybe. This life is the greatest gift we will ever receive—that we know of. It's how we use this gift that falls on us. In my life, family is everything, my greatest creation—and I have made a lot of things. And the older I grow, the greater my pride. Look what I contributed. Good people. I have done my job.

Now to more important things. You have no idea what I have been dealing with. A couple weeks before Christmas, I passed the last female on my Candy Crush playlist. Now it's just Jonathan, Baba, and me. But do I ever win a game? Rarely. And I am almost always hanging onto the bottom rung. But Christmas Day! Christmas Day, I actually won seven games!!! Merry Christmas.

I wonder if my competitors play while watching football too? I watch little TV, but I want my football. Maybe it's not the game so much as the company. I like listening for some reason.

I have a suspicion that both guys are buying boosters and extra lives. Not I. They'll see. What also makes me smile is that both have put up pictures, so I know what they look like. All they see of me is a cartoon cow head the game originally posted. Seems appropriate for a rancher, so I keep it. My goal is to post my real picture about the time I am ready to pass them just so they can see they were beaten by an old lady. But it would serve no purpose, since you never see those you pass again. Such is life.

If I go on, it will be only to rant about the plight of our country, my fear for our country. So I shall save you the grief. Though a question comes to mind: do you think of yourself as a good person? If so, why have you been good? Because as children we were exposed to hell?

Letter 22: March 2021

———— ❋ ————

On January 27, my oldest daughter was diagnosed with uterine cancer, and I knew it was the bad one because of how quickly things were moving. Yet still it felt like forever as cancer came crashing into my life once again. Then I went into extended A fib –again—and spent three days at Stanford so that they could increase my Sotalol and do a cardioversion. Though it worked on the very first try, it did little to ease my foreboding. At the same time, I began to worry that the reason I hadn't heard from you in weeks was simply because I drive you nuts. Maybe you were ill. Heart? COVID? Then yesterday came Michelle's results from UC Med Center. They got it! Everything!! No need for chemo or radiation!!! All twenty-four lymph nodes they tested were clear. They will still watch her, but the sun shines once more.

I guess why I am writing this to you is that you were interested in discussing religious convictions at some point. All I know is that it is very difficult being an agnostic. Who is there to beg when you are desperate? There is something that drives this universe, this world of ours. What, I have no idea. But I like to pretend it was her sister and father who saw her through. No matter. I feel blessed and hope you are well.

His letter arrived within days: "It makes fine sense to me that your daughter pulled through with the help of her father and her sister. And you, too." I really wanted a hug at that moment. He then shared his last moments with his mother. And that he had totaled his truck in an accident.

Then came, "I might be more mellow now because I did open your card right away—well, within a couple hours—and it didn't drive me nuts." Oh, how I would have loved to hug him that day!

Letter 23: March 2021

———— ❖ ————

You bought your last truck in 1997? Seems Henry had a good life. Almost 25 years! He obviously led a good one. And he protected you at the very end since you were not the one to die. I cannot even imagine a sandstorm that quick, that deadly. I just had a feeling, I sensed something had to be amiss. Thank you for writing back, against your better judgment, I'm sure.

Found out today Michelle had two tumors: one the size of an orange, the other the size of a golf ball. Her doctors haven't gone so far as to claim a miracle, but they throw around words like "amazed" and "lucky" over and over. I feel relieved and conflicted at the same time. I want so much to simply believe, but Michelle had a fax sent to my receiver last week where I discovered her cancer was an adenocarcinoma. The worst of the worst in my opinion. There is nothing they can do—if it has metastasized. Jack died from lung adenocarcinoma. I do believe…. Please let them be right!

Thank you for sharing what you told your mother as her death neared, that she was in your blood and in your bones. That is exactly what I was trying to express in one of my earlier letters.

That is the only reason for our time on this earth, to become a part of someone's blood, someone's bones. And those we share with carry our blood and bones onward, ever onward. Sure, Michelle has already done that. But children are not supposed to go before their parent. Especially this parent. My brother and mother both died of HCM in the early 1970s—when I was diagnosed—so why didn't I? (I'm not complaining, mind you. I had things to do.) My mother's mother outlived all five of her children. My concept of hell.

You like to wonder. Here is what has me wondering right now. Michelle was diagnosed on her brother John's and his son Jack's birthday. Of all the 365 days? Michelle also feels a connection with rainbows. She followed a rainbow all the way home from Turlock on the day she was diagnosed. A double rainbow touched down right behind our arena at the time of her vows on the day she was married. She says she saw rainbows on each of the days her sons were born. But the best rainbow in my mind came the morning she was taking her sons to school and some crazy decided it would be a good idea to commit suicide by driving headlong into a logging truck on Woods Creek Bridge—changing her mind at the last minute, thus only clipping Michelle's car. The miracle—no one was hurt. And I'll admit to seeing an uncanny number of rainbows the two weeks we waited for her surgery. But to keep all this wondering fair, Michelle is no longer married to her rainbow man. What's up with that?

Letter 24: April 2021

---※---

Glad you enjoyed the honey. Of course bees died in its making. Without a queen, there would be no honey. And the queen's only mission is to produce a zillion workers, which requires drones, whose stomachs explode after breeding her. Even worse, all her little female worker bees are rendered celibate after she fogs them with pheromones. Won't even go into those killed by automobiles.

I went to YouTube and watched the Harari/ Portman program you talk about. But I am still wondering about one of your comments. You say the truth gets lost. How can the truth get lost? Do we even know what it is? I like listening to Harari. I like how he thinks. Most of the time.

But I felt like Portman seemed to drag everything down. You worry about the audience? I barely noticed them. What is it about me that makes me feel everyone is talking directly to me? And I often argue with them.

Do you have a pet? My cat talks to herself just like I do. Gets quite interesting around here.

Young calves that are taken from their mothers at birth for milk purposes are called veal, and people love it. Do most have any idea where it originates? Probably not. What is bugging me at this moment is what I have recently read, that agriculture rates third on the list of the top five carbon producers, and I had no idea. Above cars! Lots of the problem coming from cattle like I raise. Oh, the guilt. I tell myself it must be because of feedlots. Ours are free range, dancing the side-stepping two-step.

Know the difference between me and a cow who loses her baby? A cow doesn't remember for long. Know why humans feel entitled to use animals however they want? Because the Bible tells them that animals were put on the earth to provide for them. Then there are some people who see every animal as a pet. What I like about Harari is that he sees how story (fiction) is our (humans') driving force. Very few humans are true thinkers. We need to be influenced and led. Story serves that purpose. He says there is no such thing as free will. Something I like to think about. Not sure I believe. Yet.

The reason there are seven billion of us is because like every other life form, we humans are doing what we were meant to do. Passing on our blood and bones. Keeping our genes rolling onward. Don't worry, like thousands and thousands of other species, we humans will go extinct—probably sooner than most of us imagine. And there is *no way* we humans are responsible for the majority of extinctions! Earth will then heal itself and confront her next challenge. Humans cling to a branch that only exists because dinosaurs were wiped out. But the exciting part is that some of us have a vague idea of what's going on, while most just wonder where they are going to get their next fix, be it a new car or a shot of heroin.

Speaking of cars, have you found a replacement for Henry?

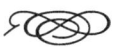

In early August, I wrote that I would be driving to Tucson the next month for a memorial, and since I would be close to where he lived, I thought I would make a side trip. I heard nothing and wondered if it meant the crash of our pen pal days—which had gone on way longer than I had ever anticipated. Then came a short note in late September asking if I had visited.

Letter 25: September 2021

---◆---

I did visit your desert community, a quick in and out. Had lunch at Carmella's (not sure I have the name right), where I had the best chimichanga I think I've ever had. A number of locals were there for a late afternoon beer, and I remember thinking what a nice community this would be for retirement living. Also saw your library. It was around 109 degrees that day, but we had recently gone through similar temps up here.

The longer we correspond, the more worthless I feel. Now you tell me that JR, your "girl" before me, got a packet of letters from you? And she sent it to you? And you are telling me about it? With more pride than frustration. How fair it that? After the browbeating I took for sending you one little paragraph? 'Tis I who should feel discomfited. She got a "packet," when all I got was a bit of writing in my yearbook. I'm teasing. All of us women tracking you down has to be good for your ego—if you would only allow it. Blame it on COVID—or old age. It makes me smile that JR was bitten by the same quest bug.

I'm looking at a picture of you posted by your Senior Center in appreciation of your service. Since I had no idea how you look today, your image came to me in many forms over this past year and a half—many not especially flattering. Age can be so uncomplimentary. I was happy to see how little you have changed. I could tell you were older, but barely.

My plan had been to take Interstate 8 to Tucson, but plans changed when I discovered that two other of my Write Sisters, who were going to attend the memorial too, needed a ride from the Phoenix airport. So, I doubled back to Interstate 10. What I enjoyed most about my side trip was seeing the Salton Sea and all those lovely date palm orchards.

I love to drive, but I have to admit I have had enough desert for a while. [I had just driven to Santa Fe back in April.]

Did I tell you my dad was living in Palm Springs when he died?

BTW, did you ever replace Henry? Stay well.

I'm sure that more than once I have mentioned how I am often impulsive. It does not scare me to do things on a whim. I can't say exactly when this idea hit me, but I think something may have been whispering before my trip to Arizona. After I came home from that trip, the whispering seemed to turn more demanding. Maybe it was because I had just met up with some of my Write Sisters in New York that month and was feeling more and more that I needed to get back to actual writing. But what I had in mind was writing like nothing I had ever written. Should I even try? Why not? Old age allows for such freedom. So off went my letter.

Letter 26: October 2021

———— ❈ ————

How would you like to collaborate with me on a book? Knowing your slant on authors, I am almost afraid to ask. But please finish reading this before you panic.

For the past year, I have had this feeling that there is something for others to 'see' in my quest. My plan was simply to put out the letters themselves with a bit of looking-back commentary. But reading back over our letters, I noticed a pattern. I was pushing into your life and having fun doing it. *Fun* might not be the correct word, but I was enjoying the anticipation, the not-knowing if I would hear from you ever again. It was my secret, since no one but Pam even knew about 'us.'

I know. I know. There was no *us*. But that is not the point. I felt giddy. Almost a schoolgirl. And at this age, it was quite enjoyable, especially since I was not in the market. But the idea of a boyfriend had its appeal. The oft-asked question, where does one find such a thing?

I don't think any of the above was intentional. But when COVID shut us down, and with the land sale, how could I not believe it was a sign?

We dated not even a year. I have come to realize that I have held about as much interest for you in your overall life as a pesky fly that's noticed for a while, only to be replaced by other flies.

Not sure when this book idea hit me, but it's been several months. Then when I was leaving your little community last month, an idea yelled at me! I had to write about what I thought versus what he (obviously) meant.

I have no problem publishing everything from my point of view, everything I wrote in my letters. And I did keep drafts, which are sort of what I wrote. So, I decided I would use them with a bit (a lot?) of commentary of what you thought I thought. When I detoured through your little community on my trip to Tucson, I had heard nothing from you in weeks and thought I never would again. I was working on the book in my head when your letter arrived, asking if I had visited and telling me about JR's mailing. Another sign? That's when the light went on. How perfect to have input from two people. What I saw on your end was how my intrusion hit you; my end, concerns (but not too serious) about what I was doing. Your belief in letter writing in a book format. What could be better than that? And don't tell me you don't have the training.

We don't have to publish. I'd be fine with you having the final say. Before the editors have the final, final say. But if I believe it is good, I will push—just so you know. Have you ever heard of a book published by old sweethearts (less than a year of dating) who have not even seen one another in over sixty years? How fun! And how cathartic—if done right. At this age, what the heck do we care what people think? I know, it's a far cry from picture books. But it could be another secret. What's more fun than that?

While waiting to hear, I began writing drafts of letters I hoped to eventually send. And as it turned out the drafts became more fun than actual letters. Was this because at the time I doubted anyone would ever see them, so I was free to say whatever I wanted?

Draft 1–October 2021

—— ❀ ——

This morning was a tough one, even though I was winning game after game. Why? Is my winning simply a false positive? My letter is sure to have reached you by today. Will you agree or won't you?

At the moment, Yo-Yo Ma is speaking to my soul. Oh, the magic of some humans, who are able to build masterpieces with simple notes, as others can do with words, and still others with a simple brush. Why, I ask again, was I skipped over? My accomplishments seem so mundane.

You asked in one of your blog posts if the industrial way proselytizes. Of course! How else could corporations and merchandising have overpowered religion? All one has to do is compare the size of cathedrals to the structures of Wall Street–both the number and sizes of buildings. I remember reading about this type of comparison decades ago, and the thought has never left my mind. Then you go on to speak of religion as though it is not a "way of life." Really?

I am now wondering if Ralph Waldo Emerson wasn't simply before his time. You quote him in a post: "Society everywhere is a conspiracy against every one of its members." Sounds to me like he would fit in nicely today. In my mind, fear is the greatest of so many of our country's problems. So much easier to believe that none of the things that scare us are true. Of course, the government is conspiring because they want us to be vaccinated. Of course, the government is going to place a chip into your arm at the vaccination site so they can know everything about you. Here's where I want to ask: do you carry a cell phone? If so, why does the government need a chip? And why would the government care what you think, unless it is you who is conspiring? I can't help but wonder if what is stirring up humanity is the threat that the end of humankind is near.

Not sure exactly what Carlin Flanagan means about a girl's elemental psychological needs being "met precisely by the art of reading." To me, we read fiction for the quest, the uncovering of what might be out there. Could any of it touch my life? That's why this girl reads anyway. Mostly I want to know what came before (worldwide before) that brought about today, that influenced history.

Where do you think your ideas originate? Anyone's ideas? No one is alone. No one is original in their thoughts. I guess there had to be original thoughts at some point. I wonder if scientists have determined how many millions of years ago that might have happened? All I know is that in this day, all builds on what has gone before. So, how "independent" does that make any writer? Which makes me wonder further: why do we put so much stock in words of those who are obviously depressed? Nay-sayers, with no proof to back them up? Comedians, who, I admit, so often seem to be spot on. Celebrities of the moment? Are their words to be believed simply because they can make hit movies? Why do we think they know of what they speak? And are researchers any better? How many theories are disproven (or not quite right) a few years down the road?

What really makes me smile is how I think of string—the same way you think of literacy. Having my degree in archaeology and all. I love literacy, not only for the knowledge and adventures, but for the placing of words to fabricate something, a something we can appreciate in exactly the way we appreciate creations made using string. String is every bit as precious to human history—before words, there was string. Maybe.

Draft 2–October 2021

———— ❈ ————

You asked once: has literacy stunted our growth? No! Again, no! As I see it, it has fertilized our growth. It has allowed for more thought. It has encouraged remembering. That's what I love about writing: "that some particular set of words makes a difference entirely on their own." To my mind, this is the most important observation you have made in your entire ten years of blogging. You go on to say, "It doesn't matter what you say; it's who you tell it to that makes all the difference." Has this always been so? Probably. Your words seem to strike a strong chord in this day of the internet.

Here is a great example of what I am talking about when I say how much I appreciate what some people can do with the same words available to anyone and everyone: "If you really want to change the world, you have to understand how it actually works and forget about punching anyone in the face." It's from Hans Roslin's book *Factfulness*. He finishes with "you have to understand how it works." But at what loss? Would any of us have remembered his words if they didn't make us think about avoiding punching anyone in the face? Sticks with you because the image is so ridiculous. Great writing! My notes say, "Dawkins should listen."

I am still not getting your difference between letters and books. Karr talks about the story "only she can tell." Isn't *her* story one that only she can tell, whether it is in a letter or a book? What am I missing?

My story is the same whether I share it with only you or with millions of others. No? But you are definitely right about us being "singular creatures." And there never would have been an *us* if we had not learned to depend on at least one other person, how to cooperate. I'm thinking you are saying we need the approval of another to be someone. I'm saying, it does not matter if others approve of you, if you don't approve of yourself. Of course, you can argue if others don't hold you in some regard, how can you? And you would be right. Though I still firmly believe no one else is going to like you if *you* don't like you. Something I have always tried to pass on to each new generation. I want so much to fix what is broken for those I love, no matter the problem. Then I ask, is this fair? Because I believe that I am what I have become because I faced life as it came with all its ups and downs. This is how we learn. I remember my grandmother telling me one time that she felt no different as an older woman than when she was seventeen until she looked in the mirror. I thought that was cute but had no concept what she was talking about. Now, with another sixty years under my belt, I think I understand. But there is a difference. We think we know everything when we are seventeen. It takes the rest of our lives to realize that no matter how long we live, we can never know everything, because everything is always changing. Life is like any other game you play. Results come from the moves you make.

Draft 3—November 2021

———— ❊ ————

It's Saturday, and as usual, I am listening to my dear friends Seth Rudetsky and Christine Pedi, whom I have never met. I'll admit it. I am a Broadway musical addict. It recently came to me why that might be. We had books and long-playing albums to entertain us growing up. No TV. My father didn't believe in it. When I close my eyes, I see covers of *Showboat, South Pacific, My Fair Lady, West Side Story, Carousel, Sound of Music,* and the list goes on.

This morning, Seth and Christine were discussing some of their favorite tunes and most came from the same shows. Strange, since there are so many shows to choose from. Suddenly it dawned on me—the albums they both admitted to "playing to death" are from musicals, based on musicals, about musicals. Of course! A perfect example of self-centeredness. Aren't we all most passionate about what matters to us? What interests us?

This leads to what I want to discuss with you today. What makes us who we are? What makes things matter to us? Why do I love ancient history and not politics? Today, Seth and

132

Christine seemed to be playing a lot of songs from *South Pacific*, and I knew every word. No wonder—*South Pacific* was a regular on our phonograph nearly every day of my growing-up years, I swear. Then it came to me: When I was seventeen, it was "Younger than Springtime" that sang to my soul. At 77, my soul hears "You've Got to be Carefully Taught." If you don't know those songs, go to YouTube and you will understand what I am talking about. Happens again with *West Side Story*. I no longer see Natalie Wood and Richard Beymer on the cover of our ancient album. Instead of searching for impossible love, I now lament humankind's unceasing social injustices. How many years has it been? Has anything changed?

Then there is *Oklahoma*, written when I was two (talk about ancient). Is it a story about corn and misunderstanding? Barely. But what do I remember every time I hear "The Surrey with the Fringe on Top"? I hear my Great-Aunt Hilda telling her surrey story. Seems a beau was clip-clopping her home in the moonlight after a dance, down a looooooooong lane. And she had to pee. Bad! Aunt Hilda described bolting from the surrey and hurdling the fence before he even had a chance to pull up to the gate. Talk about romantic.

I have a gazillion pens—most are out of ink. I have been using them to jot down my thoughts and finally throw away those that have lost their "blood." Almost makes me feel my thoughts might be good for something after all. Even if it's nothing more than cleanup.

If your answer is no, will there be any more thoughts? Guess we'll have to wait and see.

I continue to win game after game, yet I hear nothing from you, and it has been nearly two weeks since I sent my letter— more like six weeks since I sent the one before. All I am looking for is your decision: yea or nay? Am I more worried that you have no desire to collaborate, or am I more worried that winning games cannot be used as my measure of how my day will go? Here is what I have decided: I will keep writing until I do or don't hear from you. Until the book is done—one way or the other. But your take on how my intrusion affected your life—while you were making other plans—would add another dimension, don't you think? If not, you'll have to read all this in a book. Book? Letters? Have to confess, I still don't get the difference.

Draft 4—November 2021

---❊---

Here's what I am now wondering about my games. Am I winning more because it's a positive sign? Or am I winning more games because I know the games better? Are these games any different from our lives? We believe if we just figure it out, we can control. *Hmmm...* What I do know is that in these games, your ability to win is controlled. Some people believe the same with life. I am not happy with that thought. I prefer to think that life is what happens while you are making other plans. I do know that in games, winning is withheld from you until "they" want you to win, especially if you have had a good run. Your fair share? Over and over, I get to one last move with plenty of chances left. You feel sure you can pull it off. Wrong. Is it random that not one of the moves you need comes anywhere near when you need them in these situations? Time and time again? Why? They want you to buy boosters, of course.

So, here is where games diverge from life. I hope. I see no puppeteer determining the outcome in life. It is up to us, the paths we take, maybe with a few grains of what we call fate sprinkled in. I remember when beginning to play these Candy Crush games, I railed at the screen, screaming, "How can you expect me to get anywhere if you don't tell me the rules?" But like in life, rules are what you learn as you are on the journey—as you play the game. Boosters are like money. The more you have, the easier the game. Not buying that booster also has consequences. A loss knocks me back. I lose my freebies. I lose my streaks. But what happens when you have an abundance? Are you happier? Not really. You simply use them faster. Seems to me, you simply want to clear the next hurdle. Always that next hurdle. It's a game. I will buy neither lives nor boosters. Then again, there are aids you can buy in real life that are worth every penny. Vaccines come to mind. Why is it vaccines are in my mind so much?

Now I am wondering, is this how religion began? You see a sign. Things seem to line up right, sometimes in your favor, sometimes not. So, you watch. You keep track. And you begin to live according to what the signs 'tell' you. Is that what I am doing with my Candy Crush games? A couple weeks ago, I could barely win one, now I seem to be sailing right along. But I have noticed nothing life-altering . How these games play with me, keeping my hopes alive. One more sign that logic fails me? If I am simply looking for positives, why can't I be satisfied with the fact that my heart has been behaving itself for an entire week? Which then makes me wonder, how is your "wonky" heart? Every time I tell myself enough is enough, just shut up, one more thing pushes its way into my thinking.

Draft 5—November 2021

———— ❁ ————

Tried to explain to my barn cats today that it wasn't time to eat because we lost an hour last night. But I understand where they are coming from. The clock says 3:00, but it sure feels like my 4:00, beer time. Then again, it's Sunday.

The little sign I bought awhile back and turned into a postcard to share with you grabbed at me when I passed by this morning. "I wonder if clouds ever look down on us and say: 'Hey look, that one is shaped like an idiot.'" It's me. It's me. They are talking about me. I know it.

It's probably time to let this one go, but... And it fits in so nicely with your question of months ago about family—where I slapped you with the notion that we owe family. That was my feeling then. Now I'm wondering, how much?

Here is what I want to say to my family at the moment. Family, believe it or not, on most things, I care not one iota how you live your lives! COVID is not one of them. So, I had to wonder why, and here is what I have come up with. To me, there is a huge difference between being vaccinated and not being vaccinated. Why do I care who is vaccinated? I care because I am self-centered. You care about what you believe because you are self-centered. Every single human is self-centered. It's the only way any of us sees, the only way we can relate to our world.

Family, I love all of you dearly. But do I love you more than myself? The things I've done—for you—I thought, was to make you happy. But now I am wondering, do I do it because it makes *me* feel good? And another thought, how much do I actually owe you? Wasn't that debt taken care of when I made possible your being? Here is what I think this all boils down to: your self-centeredness vs. my self-centeredness. As I see it, because of you, my unvaccinated kin, and all those who will not get vaccinated, I cannot travel the way I want to travel. Yes, we could have our family gatherings, vaccinated and unvaccinated, with the unvaccinated simply testing. But that is not the point.

Not sure how I feel about this imposed mandate though. I want people to decide for themselves what I see as the best choice—self-centeredness at its best. What I do know is that I have no desire to gather with a disagreeing family during the holidays. COVID may be on the decline. Or is it? And we humans are not helping the cause. This nasty little virus leaves its mark on other things besides bodies. The point to me is that if everyone in the world who doesn't have a real medical issue would simply get their vaccines, COVID could be over before we know it. Whose dream is it to live in the slums? Is COVID any different? As I see it, this is what a vaccinated body becomes to a virus. A slum. Not a desirable place to multiply.

I have been told that because my anti-vaccine grandchildren are only in their twenties, I should act like the adult. I have also been told that I get into peoples' lives "all the time." I've also been told that I don't get involved enough. What can I say? I'm self-centered. One thing I *have* learned: I will never again send a family group text.

Do they have the right to scold me? Of course they do, but I would suggest that they never do anything before considering unforeseen consequences—one of the main things we teach our children but rarely heed ourselves. I need to be aware that my reaction in all likelihood will also produce unforeseen consequences.

It is not our difference of opinion that has me rattled. It was the unexpected attack. Consequences, pure and simple. I think I may be onto something here. Do we sometimes screw up our own lives, pushing what we think is good for others? I am beginning to realize how truly judgmental I am. How right is this for someone who professes (and believes) that it is every adult's right to build their own right—what is right for them. I add too much drama to everything. Because I am a writer... Who needs it? Life has plenty already.

The best way to treat the problem is to step back—to keep my mouth shut. So that is what I am going to try to do. How likely is this to happen? I can hear what you are thinking: *not likely*. We shall see. So now, I am planning another just-me holiday. This is more appealing to me than the thought of a house full of forced merriment. How long will it be to see how this family survives COVID?

Know what else I was wondering today? Generation after generation, we criticize how things were done before, including how we were raised. Each generation strives to raise their kids better than they were raised. What are we saying? That there is something wrong with us? And taking from Broadway one more time, this time *Jesus Christ Superstar:* "There have been poor always pathetically struggling, look at the good things you've got." I can't help but wonder if the word *at* shouldn't be changed to *for*: "Look for the good things you've got." Many humans have all sorts of good things—"I've got the sun in the mornin' and the moon in the evenin'" (from yet another Broadway play) comes to mind. We simply have to see. That's why I wanted you to work on this book with me. But who am I to decide your good? Do I simply think it would be good for you because I see it as being good for me?

Do you remember "Desiderata" on the pop charts in the late 1970s? I must have remembered it more than I thought because when I dug it up today, I realized that everything it says is what I have been trying to say in my letters to you. The reason I was looking for it today was because words from this poem helped me through my Gina days. They were also what gave me the clout to let an employee who was really getting on my nerves go when I owned Here's the Scoop. The phrase goes, "Avoid loud and aggressive persons, for they are vexations to the spirit." What I remembered was avoid *irritating* persons, for they are vexations to the *soul*. I still go by my version. And that is exactly why I let her go, though I told her it was because we could never be on the same page. Same thing?

This poem was written in 1927 by Max Ehrmann, but so much of it is still resonates. "Nurture strength of spirit to shield you in sudden misfortune. But do not stress yourself with dark imaginings." Aren't a lot of the nay-sayers of today distressed by dark imaginings?

Still trying to put this one into perspective: "Take kindly the counsel of years, gracefully surrendering the things of youth." Have I screwed up major here? Then again, when I translate this sentence, I think it must be saying, some things you can no longer do—live with it! Always remembering, "You are a child of the universe no less than the trees and the stars," though definitely not here as long. But then again, we have every "right to be here" even when acting like a teeny-bopper in our old age. Right?

I have barely been able to shed a tear since Gina died. But every time I hear Jean Valjean singing his swan song in *Les Misérables*, my eyes water. Is it because he recognizes that he was not always right? Makes me wonder and guilty at the same time.

I don't think I have told you that I own a meat processing plant with four other ranchers. After the first six months of COVID, I decided to begin making pies to sell there because someone just happened to say, "Too bad you don't have pies, then I would have the perfect meal." I had given up my cottage license when I was spending all my time traveling. So, I renewed the cottage license I had gotten after I closed Here's the

Scoop. I know pies. I made hundreds at the Scoop. And I like to make them—when I'm not traveling. This morning I was thinking, *Maybe this is one more reason I am not feeling devastated about another year of alone for the holidays.* My girls and daughter-in-law are fabulous cooks and bakers. We always have way more than we need because everyone can and likes to make. Not so in every home. My customers especially like my pies because they have to bake them. I sell them unbaked and frozen, so they feel they have a step in the production. And they are completely made from scratch in my home. A homemade pie!

A little more about Rawhide Meats. I had found a way to sell our ranch meat at my ice cream parlor. Actually, it was sold in the side I called Locals Make Good. At that time, we had to transport the cattle we wanted to use four hours north so they could be USDA killed, inspected, and processed. In the meantime, we attended meetings at our University Extension Service to learn how else we might be able to sell farm-to-table. Now here's the lucky part, which crops up in my life time after time. There was only one processing plant in our entire county when we learned at a meeting, if you own your own processing plant and your own business, you can sell your meat through that business—if the animals are USDA inspected at kill. Here's the magic: guess what plant went on the market at that exact time? So, we bought it, four ranchers—three men and four women. At the end of 2018, we lost two of our men, but Dick skates right along in this female-dominated partnership. Two years ago, in a proud moment, he brought in his son. So often, these types of partnerships do not work. Once again, I feel blessed.

Tricia's Herd—of cats

Mama Pig caring for her little ones

Draft 6—November 2021

———◈———

A few minutes ago, I watched a race between "my" flock of wild turkeys and my pigs. Not sure what the pigs thought they were going to get. They are fed their supplements in the morning. The turkeys, on the other hand, make their rounds about this time every day. They love the pomegranates that have split open and spilled their seeds. I think the pigs are simply jealous because the turkeys are able fly over the fence to grab whatever tasty treats they want, while the pigs can do nothing but watch. On top of that, the chickens got the apple peels from the pie apples today. Perhaps tomorrow will be a better day for the pigs. Seems everyone has to wait and see sometimes.

Since we are on the subject of pigs....our pigs run in a field, eating lots of grass and acorns. Well, I'm not sure about grass, probably more roots, but I do know that they tear the crap out of our fields—that's why we run them in only two fields. But what I wanted to share is how great farrowing time is. The mother flops down. The babies are born and hide under the grass for the first couple days. Then, here they come like puppies. Wish I could send you pictures, but of course I don't have your cellphone number. The babies eat whenever, and from whichever mother, they want. They are the only animals as a species that I have seen who seem not to care who is suckling. I have always talked about how animals have no judgment when it comes to skin color. But they do care about species, sticking mostly with their own.

I bring this up because I loved watching last winter when we had some really cold days. We hold some bulls in the same field as our pigs. The pigs would stand around watching until a bull lay down, then off they scurried to snuggle up for warmth, usually only one or two pigs per bull. I loved this blending of the them and us. Listening to South Pacific with Seth and Christine this morning, then watching various ads to get free boosters in my games, I couldn't help but wonder, are we nearing a time when all humans will look alike? Then it comes to me, there are lots of really skinny and really fat people. Will we ever average that out? And if we do, it means nothing more than we will have to find something else to drive the them versus us. But I still remember a time when there was nothing but white on our television screens, then came a bit of Sammy Davis, Jr., Bill Cosby, and sometimes Ella Fitzgerald and Lena Horne. They gave us so much. One step forward, two steps back. No wonder we never get very far.

Been thinking (again?) about your obsession with letter writing. Is this not a forerunner to the nurturing of global interaction? People getting to know people around the world. I think I have known that people are basically the same everywhere since I was very young. I feel I always understood the importance of people getting to know people from around the world. I grew up with a far-right conservative grandmother on one side and a very liberal Democrat grandmother on the other. No matter, I hated politics since my father lost an election for District Attorney when I was ten. But what I have never forgotten is my one grandmother calling me a communist about that time because I had said that what Russian leaders were doing was not the fault of her people.

I was reading something recently about humans being the only animals to blush, to feel shame. How much good has that done us? Back in the day, when I was watching the news, I simply skipped over things that made me uncomfortable: starving children, raped women, puppy mills. What could I do to change these horrific situations? They claimed I could fix it with money. Now a different they is saying the same thing about fixing our climate problems.

I track all this back to something Bergman says in Humankind: A Hopeful History when he tells us that the best way to imagine humankind is to put us where we belong, and he uses a single year—January to December—to represent the span of four billion years that life has inhabited our planet. According to him, up until October, "bacteria had the place to themselves." And probably some nasty viruses. Then in November, here comes something we might just be able to see: "buds and branches, bones and brains." Humans probably came on the scene at about 11:00 p.m. that last night but did not get around to inventing farming until about 11:59 p.m. See what that means? Everything I have studied in ancient history never happened until the final sixty seconds of that year. Everything we know of history!!! And yet so many of us believe we know it all.

Draft 7—November 2021

———— ❁ ————

Last night as I was falling asleep, it dawned on me that I have never caught you up on several ramblings I made early in our correspondence. The first is that I have had absolutely no contact with my college roommate Chris since those first two lunches. What is the saying? The road is paved with good intentions. Unfortunately, it seems that at least one of any two needs to be willing to do the paving. And I have to ask, did you ever get around to watching Betty Buckley singing "Old Flame" on YouTube as I suggested? Did it help at all as an example of how screwy we women can be at times? Not my exact autobiography, no matter what you think. But she is spot-on on one thing—you can't always trust Google for addresses.

My next revelation is much more interesting. Remember me wondering about Kunta Kinte? Could someone from my family have owned him? Well, my research shows that someone from my family was the owner mentioned in the 2020 PBS miniseries Roots, but I am not a direct-line descendant. The owner mentioned in the series was John Waller. That's what caught my ear because I had recently been working on that branch of my family tree, which contained several John Wallers. From what I have now figured out, both my seventh and eighth great-grandfathers were John Wallers but neither could have owned Kunta Kinte because they were both dead by the time he arrived in America. But my seventh great-grandfather also had a son, John Waller (1712-–76). According to what is written on Ancestry.com, it was this John Waller who owned Kunta Kinte. His sister Winifred is my sixth great-grandmother, making John my sixth great-uncle. No sigh of relief here. As I see it, this does not absolve my family from wrongdoing, for I am sure my many-greats grandfather also owned slaves.

Bergman claims the days of slavery are over, but are they? After watching a bunch of criminal justice programs, it seems slavery may never be over, so long as there are people willing to pay: young women to fill fantasies, children to work in your house. What is wrong with us? "What's the use of wonderin'?" is what Julie Jordan asks in Carousel. Not wondering about what needs to be wondered is what we humans seem to be best at. Is that because we have been warned and warned that curiosity killed the cat? But unlike Julie, I wonder. I wonder where our world would be if we humans were never curious? We've come a long way in that last minute of Bergman's year. But what if we hadn't wondered? Would we still be frolicking in our Garden of Eden?

Think about it. Would that have meant there would never have been a Pet Rock? Yikes. Do you remember the Pet Rock? It made Gary Dahl a millionaire. And what was it? A rock.

Not even a decorated rock, though each did have a couple glue-on eyes and came with how-to-care-for-your-pet instructions. Not to mention the clever packaging. What I wonder is how many millions of dollars were lost by copycats trying to imitate Dahl's cleverness? I know—I tried "what-if" things a time or two.

Do you remember the Golden Chain, Highway 49? I think it went right by the front door of your house. Well, it cuts through the middle of our ranch about fifteen miles further south, a major tourist highway. It's been closed for over ten days. The state finally decided to fix a major flooding problem caused by a seasonal creek that floods the highway every year or so. When we moved down to this ranch about fifty-seven years ago, there was hardly a car on the road. Then came the logging trucks. Then came commuters from up Yosemite way. Then came fearing for your life every time you walked across the road to get your mail. The problem was the closure was town-side just above John's and my houses, which added about eleven miles each way when we went to town. Plus, no mail delivery the first few days (not that I expected to find a letter from you anyway). It took barely a day for us to appreciate the road closure, no matter the inconveniences. It was so quiet. And the guys were able to move cattle across the road without having to truck them. I cannot remember how long it has been since they could actually move cattle across the road without someone flipping us off or stopping in the middle of the herd to take pictures. Long gone is the cattle drive from ranch to ranch in this part of the world. But this wasn't all. My daughter-in-law Sarah picked up trash on both sides of the highway all along the road closure plus trimmed all along the highway side of the corrals. Looking good around here. For a while. Being typical ranchers, though, we can't simply appreciate how great the grass is growing this fall. Perfect temperatures. Just the right amount of rain. Cows are happy!! But the grass is also coming back where Sarah trimmed and other places we don't want it.

Draft 8—November 2020

———◆———

Have you ever thought about how amazing technology advances were during our grandparents' lives? It has always filled me with such wonder, not to have things then to have them as an expected part of your life: automobiles, airplanes, radios, television, phonographs, telephones, credit cards, and on and on. But what about our lives? We are now the grandparents, and we take so much for granted that it is difficult to even remember what we once didn't have. When you lived in Tuolumne County, we were barely seeing an increase in traffic on our main Sonora street, Washington. We new drivers would spend hours dragging main and could afford to because 19 cents per gallon for gas was on the high side in those days. How many long distance phone calls did you get in those days? Not many, I'm guessing. To call thirty miles away was long distance and cost a fortune. Now we can hook up with friends almost anywhere in the world, and it costs us nearly nothing.

I remember my mom double-parking on Washington Street while she ran into the grocery store to pick up a gallon of milk. Can anyone from this generation even imagine? Can they imagine a time without cellphones? Without computers? And now we wear watches that can do almost anything a cellphone can. Yeah, we knew about these watches back then. At least 60 years ago. Dick Tracy wore one. But could we even imagine wearing one as part of daily attire? Which reminds me, some watches can be irritatingly bossy with their reminders: stand up, time to sleep, and my favorite, breathe. What the heck does it think I've been doing?

When I first began writing in the mid-eighties, we thought we were in heaven with our electric typewriters. But we were still using carbon paper and whiting out our mistakes. Still kicking myself for getting rid of my first computer, a Tandy 1000. More a word-processor than a computer. I told Jack I would never need another thing. How I loved how easy it made writing. And it had these wonderful 5x5 disks on which to store your stories. Still have the disks, but have no idea how to get into them to read them. Good thing I kept hard copies too. You also needed a similar disk to boot it up. Every time. So, three months later, I wanted something newer, of course. Typical of almost any technical development of humankind, don't you think? Were our grandparents any different? From a wall phone you had to crank to a princess phone. From horse and buggy to Corvette.

I can still remember my first introduction to email. My Write Sister, Mary, worked for a school district and told me if I went up to our school district office, I could send her a letter that she would get immediately. Sounded fascinating, but I never got around to trying before it became possible for me to do so from my own home. Nothing like today, but amazing compared to yesterday. Around that same time, there was a commercial on the Super Bowl, back when Super Bowl commercials were something to watch. It still brings goosebumps when I think of it. And none of us had a clue what it meant. We just liked seeing it. It featured the young child actor from *The Piano*. She was walking away from us through this expansive green field, then she turns and whispers, "It's coming. The super-highway is coming." Huh? Now we cannot even imagine that there was a time we lived without the internet.

What's next? I think it's already here. Crypto. Can you imagine a digital or virtual currency "that is secured by cryptography which makes it nearly impossible to counterfeit or double-spend?" I learned about it on the internet. Haven't a clue what they are talking about. Sounds too good to be true, like so many of our human inventions. Oh, the minds that figure out these kinds of things. Again, I ask, why was I skipped over, though I guess I should be satisfied that I can at least figure out how to use some of the inventions that have made our lives so much easier. And more stressful, don't you think?

I've reached the point that I no longer anticipate finding a letter from you in my mailbox, and I will soon have to make a decision. Then I realized that when one game seemed to be lugging down, the other two kept chugging along. Maybe all is not lost? Yet.

Draft 9—November 2021

———◆❁◆———

I see I keep talking about my Write Sisters. How could I not? They have become so important in my life. So now you get to hear about how and why I started writing. The why is easy. It was just something I always wanted to do. And what training did I have? None! Except that my English teachers all seemed to like how I put words on a page, just like that editor I told you about so long ago. So, I signed up for a creative writing class at our community college. It was my instructor who asked if I had ever thought about writing for children. At that point, I hadn't gotten that far. Simply decided it was time to write.

Remember, at this time, there was no internet. I think I discovered SCBW (The Society of Children's Book Writers) in a copy of *The Writer's Digest* I found at the library, and they were having a conference in August. This was a year before they changed their name to SCBWI (throwing illustrators into the pot). What was unexpected was that the minute I walked through the door into that conference room, I knew this was where I belonged. I never missed a conference for the next twenty years. That's where I met Mary, the first of my Write Sisters. She and I attended the same critique session where we could read our stories. I liked hers. She liked mine. And fate put us right next to each other on our bus ride to the airport. The speaker that year was the editor who would buy my first book. I think I had been writing for less than two years when I sold *Just Like My Dad*. But I have already told you that story. I thought, *What a cinch*. Riiiight.

The good news was that because I had sold a book, I qualified to attend a Jane Yolen conference in Port Townsend, Washington. I think that's where I met Ann, even though she lived in Los Angeles, and I am sure she had to have been at that first SCBW conference I attended, though I can't swear to it, depending only on my memory. The rest is hazy, and none of us quite agree. I think it was the next year when I asked Ann if she would ever consider holding a small critique session at her home around or during the conference. She said, why not? I had not the slightest idea where her home might be. At that time, I barely knew Los Angeles. Then there it was in the Los Feliz district, to the right and below the Hollywood sign, a 1930s-era home snuggled in a magnificent compound. I have always felt like Nancy Drew (my first binge series) the minute I cross the threshold into that house. It was at this first critique session where I heard and saw picture books that were newly out or would be coming out soon, all written by new friends. And I wanted to tell the world about these books.

When I got home that year, I went to our local newspaper and made a deal with publisher/owner Harvey McGee. I would write a weekly about newly published picture books, for nothing, which I would call *Picture This*, if he would contribute an annual sum towards bringing children's book authors into our schools. Not quite telling the world, but I loved what I was doing. I can proudly boast that I never missed a week in all ten years writing the column. And my Write Sisters were the first and last children's authors I brought for author visits into our county.

Little did I know that publishers from all houses would be sending me books once I began my column. If I remember right, I donated around 3,000 books to Jamestown Elementary (where both my children and grandchildren attended) after I opened my ice cream parlor and gave up the column. And, of course, eventually the books I reviewed were not all written by friends. My Write Sisters loved the books I dragged down year after year. A few years had passed since our first critique session at Ann's. Our invitation list had shrunk. There are only so many manuscripts that can be critiqued in a day. After a few years, it was the same seven of us—year after year. And did I mention that we now spent three days at Ann's before each conference? One big pajama party. I think the reason they put up with me is that every year I brought down the books I had been sent. Almost as soon as I got there, books lay piled and strewn across Ann's living room floor and remained there until we gathered them up and shoved them back into my car before we headed off to the conference. A never-changing scene for all the years I reviewed.

One year we decided our group needed a name. Several were tossed around, then I suggested the Write Sisters. I loved all the ways to play the words. My sisters are now spread all across the U.S. as sisters often are. But what I love best about them is that they took me back after I had not written a word in twenty years. They may not have been on my speed dial during that time, but they never left my heart. Remember what I told you earlier, that once someone makes me care about them, it does not matter how much time has passed, to me it was just yesterday that we parted. There is not room here to list all their successes and talents, so Google them and you will see what I am talking about. My Write Sisters: Mary Nethery, Ann Paul, Kirby Larson, Helen Ketteman, Vivian Sathre, Dian Curtis Regan, and me, their Cinderella stepsister.

I'm sure you remember my two other sisters. Pam was a freshman when we dated, Tina was in seventh grade. I still marvel at how three type-A personalities survived under the same roof for all those years and were able to remain friends. Maybe because I am the only one who remained in the area? Pam became a single mother and basically raised her kids doing craft fairs, though she had a teaching credential. Tina also did the craft fair circuit for years, though hers was a military family who moved around the world. People loved her bread dough ornaments and jars, and she made more money in a single show than Pam and I combined for the season. I often wonder, where did we get such drive? Such need to produce? They say look to the parents. Good idea.

Our dad was an attorney who built houses for a hobby—in the evenings and on weekends. If I remember right, he built seven in all: the one I grew up in, the one the family moved into right after I got married, the one for my grandparents, and the few after my mother died. Our mother was a singer, as you remembered in your first letter. She sang with and for everyone. Her talent gene seems to have skipped over all five of her children. Pam definitely got Dad's building gene. To date, she has flipped about twenty houses and is still at it.

Draft 10—November 2021

———— ❖ ————

This morning, I watched a woodpecker trying to figure out where to get to work on one of the many metal pipes we now use as fence posts. Around and around he hopped as he searched for just the right place to begin his quest. Is this what I am doing? Attempting an impossible feat? Can we ever know ourselves? Along with the watching, I was listening to my Dueling Divas, Seth and Christine, On Broadway. Know what this means? Another week has passed with still no word.

Also, this morning I awoke with "People, people who need people are the luckiest people in the world" banging around in my brain. I know I told you about these songs that I wake up hearing. Where they come from, and for what reason, I'm not sure. Now I'm wondering, are they? Are people who need people the luckiest people in the world? Haven't we all seen what mass gatherings can lead to? How they can corrupt what we see as the most caring of humans. And what do we mean by *need*?

I thought I needed you for input, companionship, through this project. Now I'm wondering if perhaps I am not better off without. Need is such a driving, controlling force. You might need a plumber. Someone to cut those branches you cannot reach. Someone to advise—though would I ever listen? When you can't do it yourself, you usually have to wait. And wait. And wait. I cannot imagine life without the people I care about, but how much do I really need them? Am I bowing my neck because I know the time is coming when I will probably have to depend on them and I'm simply sidestepping—for as long as possible.

One thing I have learned is that you can't do everything at the same time and expect to get anything done. I think that's the reason I binge. It might be rugs. Then I put them away, pull out my knitting, and crank out a few sweaters. Toddler sweaters, but still sweaters. Or I might read twenty books in a row. But writing, when you put it away, it may be for a long, long time. And I have come to realize that eats at your gut, if you are a real writer. The best part? You can always write, no matter what else you are doing. Which brings me back to an earlier comment when I said that opening Here's the Scoop may have been a good thing because it brought me back.

Have never been in analysis. Might be interesting. Why is it I hate to waste even a minute of time? Is it perhaps because I was only thirty-three when I was diagnosed with HCM and believed I didn't have a minute to spare? After all, my mother and brother had both died of sudden-death within the previous four years. I remember worrying that my young children might come home on the bus to find their mother cold on the kitchen floor. My first goal was to see each of them graduate from elementary school. To this day, part of me believes that this is what has kept me forging ahead all these years—my goals. "I don't have time to die quite yet because I haven't finished such and such." This is where I should probably mention how far they have come in understanding HCM with their ICDs and all those wonderful medicines. Now I'm a great-grandmother. And I still feel—EVERY DAY—that I am not doing quite enough. But there is still so much on my to-do list. No wonder I drive people crazy.

Is this my problem? Is this why I don't feel I do enough? Yes, I am self-centered. But now I am thinking I am also selfish. I am more selfish with my time than I am with my money. I have no problem taking several stars off the Christmas tree at the bank for the needy each year. I don't even begrudge the time it takes to buy and wrap the gifts, so long as it isn't too much time. But how often will you find me volunteering? And while I'm at it, I've been wondering, do people accomplish more today because of all the apps they are now able to download? Seems to me less and less gets done because of all the time everyone spends on their apps, the internet in general. Don't get me wrong, there is definitely a place. That's why I love the internet. The time it saves. Especially the time it has saved me.

Draft 11—November 2021

I was nineteen when Jack and I married. Remember, at that time we knew nothing about our prefrontal cortex not being fully developed at that age, so of course I thought I knew everything I needed to know. About everything. That first year we lived on the home ranch in a mobile home halfway between his folks and his grandmother. I remember exactly where I was standing on our front porch when we got the news that President Kennedy had been shot. That's what I remember most about my first home as Mrs. Gardella.

That coming spring, Uncle Joe died, and we moved down to the Montezuma ranch which Joe had cobbled together in the 1920s buying up abandoned mining claims. I thought I had died and gone to heaven. Joe was a bachelor and had lived in his old gray house for nearly fifty years. The kitchen contained a pie cabinet and an ancient wood cook stove. The walls were black with soot. Almost forgot, there was also a not-quite-so-ancient unplugged electric stove under one window. Story goes that Joe set his sweater on the stove before turning on a burner, or before allowing the burner to cool. Joe never used that stove again. The sink for the kitchen could be found somewhere on the back porch room. I swear, if you were strong enough, you could have wrung water from the wood that comprised the drain board. At one point, there had apparently been a linoleum countertop, but most of it had worn away, probably before either Jack or I were born. One day, I dragged my mom down to see my new abode. I loved it! Vines covered nearly every inch of both stories and seemed determined to decorate the interior as well. Mom looked around. "Never in my life could I imagine anyone wanting to live in something...something like this."

Wasn't long before we had that place pretty shipshape, I thought. Of course, there were a few things we simply ignored, like the linoleum in the kitchen floating high off the floor whenever the wind blew. I guess we should have tacked it down. Then there was honey that dripped from the living room ceiling whenever it got hot. Darn honey can really hide in the cracks. We thought we had done a good job cleaning out that huge beehive beneath the upstairs bedroom floor. After we got the cats, the mouse population seemed to decrease. And we barely noticed the bats rattling in our bedroom wall as they made their way in and out each night.

All four of my children were born while we lived there, and I had a convenience few other parents can boast. Our kitchen floor had about a 6% grade, I'd say, so when my little ones were in their walkers, I could keep them entertained while I made dinner by kicking them back up the 'hill' after they had made their way to the counter where I was working. Today, that house is around 170 years old and looks better than ever. That's what face-lifts can do—when done right. But I've seen what they can do when done wrong. One of the reasons I would never be tempted.

John was almost two when we moved into our new home across the "street" (Hwy 49) at the top of Piety Lane. We paid less for our house than an SUV costs today. Did I tell you that in 1850, nearly 900 people lived in our town? I guess the gold was so plentiful in the flats in 1849 that you could literally pick up chunks. When John was in eighth grade, he had to write a history paper. He was going to write it on the San Francisco Giants or some such, but his teacher talked him into writing it about the townsite of Montezuma. This was before I started writing, but I helped him, part of which meant taking him around to interview a few residents who had been in the area almost back to Gold Rush days. I think his paper was about seven pages when he finished it. Mine was probably closer to thirty pages—and that was before internet research. Can you imagine what I could find today using Google? Maybe this will be the year I revise it, as I have promised myself I would for nearly forty years.

It was a good thing we moved down to Montezuma when we did. Well, maybe there was no rush, but twenty years later, a Big Five was sitting right where our mobile home had once stood with Walmart and other strip-mall businesses in the Crossroads Junction too. A few years before that, CalTrans had cut Sonora Bypass right through the middle of our original ranch. (I say *our*, though I have only been part of the family for 58 years.) But Jack, his siblings, and his parents (both only children) are all gone. The only Gardellas left from this line originate with me, which I feel gives me license.

I hear you. You are saying, *Way too often you think things give you license.* I know, I pushed into your life. And I truly don't know—do you think I've made it hell?

There's a Lowe's commercial that keeps coming up on my game boards: "It isn't chestnuts roasting that brings the family together. It's you." And the guilt begins to flow once more. I am supposed to be the well-aged adult. Was I any different? My mother's horror at my residence preference probably says it all. But I never attacked my elders. We respected authority even when we didn't always agree. This may be what is bothering me the most. I felt attacked. Verbally. And I am trying hard to see if this falls on my shoulders. But because I live by the tenet that "life is what happens while you're making other plans," shouldn't I just take things as they come? Even when things could be easily prevented?

Yes, I'm back to vaccines. Tuolumne County is going through a terrible upsurge in recent COVID cases. The majority of those hit are unvaccinated, but several totally vaccinated people have died. Would these vaccinated people have contracted the disease if everyone had been vaccinated? I don't know. But once again, I go back to my slums analogy. If we make it tougher for the virus to survive, won't that decrease the number of viruses, and won't this increase the survival chance of those we care about? Makes sense to me. But I was thirty-five before it dawned on me that not everyone thinks like me.

Artwork of the house Tricia and Jack moved into

Draft 12—November 2021

———— ❋ ————

What if there was a way we could find out everything our lives held in store for us? Would you want to know? Think about it. At least you would have had a heads-up that I was coming.

Not I. I love the mystery, the twists, the turns. Back in the day, we never imagined there was a way we could know the gender of our baby before it was born. I try to imagine how different the birth of my fourth would have been. I was positive *she* was another girl. The doctor said *she* would be a small girl. And I was fine with that. That being said, I can still feel the volcano erupting when I heard, "It's a boy!" And what a boy! Ten pounds, one-and-a-half ounces. His father was sure he could put him to work in about a week.

I keep going back to Google saying there are no twenty-first-century thinkers. What the heck does that mean? That no one is sharing their thoughts as Bertrand Russell did? "Never let yourself be diverted by what you wish to believe." Does one need a degree in philosophy to be rated a thinker? How dare I wonder if my thoughts have any place among those of the thinkers of this time? How does one know when one knows?

What about writers for Broadway? I think they think. And I like how many of them think. Even if I don't always agree. Am I being diverted? Here I go again. It's okay not to agree with Broadway, but it's not okay not to agree with family. *Get over it*. But will I?

Blame it on Broadway. Do you think Broadway has become my religion? I could almost put together a bible of how humans should behave using nothing but Broadway verses. Maybe it had nothing to do with COVID—my quest. Maybe it came because of how Don Quixote sings about marching into hell for a heavenly cause. Maybe I simply wanted one too. A cause. A quest. He asks, would the world be better if we stay "true to our glorious quest? To reach the unreachable stars." Sounds so romantic. I believe it is perfectly fine to reach for the stars, so long as you appreciate the view and the treetops as you pass. That which has already come to be.

I did not begin this quest because I thought I needed you. Just thought it might be fun. I guess I thought we would reminisce about the old days. Hard to do when neither of us can remember much about them.

Do fantasies ever work the way we imagine? This one certainly didn't.

Two more weeks—that's all you get. If I don't hear from you by then, I go it alone. Sorry it has to be without you, but it is done. Time to move on. On all counts.

For some reason, the Fates did not want us to meet again. I should have known better. How often have I heard you can never go back? But several of my friends have done just that and seem to be enjoying it so much. Could it be because they didn't do it the same way I have? Or could this be because a book needed to be written? And I didn't know. Another detour. Another case of the Fates stepping in? Stranger still is that I no longer envision only you as I write. I see many. Readers all. Curious readers like me. You wrote in your very first letter to me, when I asked if you wanted to be my pen pal, "My turn, your turn, my turn again, till death do us part?" I told you then not to worry, that I would probably soon be onto another quest. Seems that "soon" has come. After all, "Life is what you do while you're waiting to die. This is how time goes by." (from *Zorba the Greek*) So, we each do what we have to do to keep going. Because I think the way I think, does this put pressure on others?

I find communicating with the world quite challenging when I (my mind) is elsewhere. Can they tell I'm not there? That's when I understand the real reason against solitude. Way too much time to spend searching. For oneself. Even when you need nothing, you need something. That's the problem with life. I believe I care deeply about *some* others. Do I? Or is it all about me? My needs. Maybe that's why I relate to cats. They do as they please. They love their offspring. They seek out company as needed. And they don't give a shit. It is what it is. But unlike a cat, I *need* to give thanks, to throw it forth, praying it lands where it belongs. I *know* there is somewhere it belongs, just have no idea where. When I look at the world, I see its light. Then I add people to the equation...

Are we humans the cracks Cohen is talking about when he sings "There's a crack in everything. That's how the light gets in."? Can we ever get any further than ourselves? Do words work at all, no matter that millions have heard them? And there have been thousands written and sung throughout our 'minute' of time.

Not sure I believe in reincarnation. But what does it hurt to think about it? What does it hurt to wonder? About the universe. About God. About our souls? What is a soul other than a storage place for wonder? When we die, we discover either we were right or we were wrong. Just like we lived. Once again, I have no clue where I am headed—except out. Are there more detours? Goals? I try to make sure that all my ducks will be in a row before I go, but I hear something...something whispering, what's your goal?

I wonder about a lot of things while at the same time being filled with such wonder. It has been fun being a human. So many options. I pray that our species can hang around for at least a couple more of Bergman's minutes. But again, life is what happens while we are making other plans. Imagine the world today if that meteor hadn't hit Central America. We mammals would probably be nothing more than dinosaur fodder. So, give thanks. We are what we are, even if it's not perfect.

Draft 13—November 2021

—❈—

I'm one of those people who can't seem to get rid of a thing. But it's not my fault. What if I need it? That's why my linen closet is stuffed with worn-out sheets. And I've never slept in most of them. Can I help it if everyone started giving me their old sheets when they found out I was using sheets in my rugs? And yarn. And other fabric. Why would I get rid of them? I might need just that color.

This is how it has been since my sister and I opened our first business back in 1974. That is when I learned my attention held about three years—until I started writing. Before the bypass, before Crossroads Junction Shopping Center, there was a little building that had once been a lumber yard office on a parcel my in-laws rented out on our home ranch. Here, Pam and I opened a ceramics studio, a great gathering place for both young and old. Unfortunately, Pam's husband got transferred. I would have to do it all now. That's when my guilt swelled out of control. How could I be a good mother, always working? My solution? I dragged my five kilns home to my garage to make and market macrame beads for the next couple years. Then Mom died. I was diagnosed. And I retired. That lasted about two weeks.

The good news was that my friend Judy had recently opened a gift shop and needed stuff. I had lots of stuff for making stuff. Unfortunately, it wasn't all the right stuff. So, of course, I had to buy more stuff. And if it's on sale, you'd better stock up on all that good stuff. One of the items I made for her was a sort-of rattle—fluffy and crocheted around a plastic egg filled with rice, I think. Cute. Simple. So, I made a larger one to fit the 1800s theme of Columbia State Park. This Drimble (as I dubbed them) sported an old-fashioned sunbonnet and looked pretty cute sitting on the gift shop shelf. I decided to make more. Then one night, just as I was drifting off to sleep, an idea struck, as ideas often do. The little Drimble was a rattle. What if I made my larger Drimble into a music box? I had music box workings left over from my ceramic days and one of them just happened to be "You Are My Sunshine." What could be more perfect for a sun-bonneted pioneer? I sewed it in. Could there be anything more perfect? Guess not. In about two days my Pioneer Drimble sold, and she was the first of a couple thousand I would sell over the next several years.

What a ride. Our Drimbles sold in all the major gift markets across the country. These things were hand-crocheted. There was no way Jack and I could do it all ourselves. He had turned into my accessory-cutter when he wasn't ranching. I put an ad in our local paper and got something like 150 applications. I hired fifteen women who came every Monday to bring what they had finished and pick up more yarn. This was about

1980, and I am still using Drimble yarn in some of my rugs, even after donating bags of yarn to senior centers and the like.

Each Drimble played a song to go with its personality. The nurse played "Spoonful of Sugar." The fireman played "Smoke Gets in Your Eyes." The dragon played "Puff the Magic Dragon." So, of course, I had to buy more music boxes. I had designed over fifty different personalities by the time I put Drimbles aside and began writing. I'm thinking there are still a number of music boxes up there in the shop buried amongst my stuff.

We were featured on television. We were approached by the producer of the Casper the Friendly Ghost cartoon. He wanted to use Drimbles in a cartoon. Drove all the way to Los Angeles to meet with attorneys. Someone else wanted to use them on sheets, t-shirts, and other paraphernalia. Most exciting of all, someone offered to buy my business. And it was a great offer.

Here is when I first began to learn about business. Jack had always been

our business head. I could almost hear him cringe when I said that I felt selling my Drimbles would be like selling one of my family. But he let me make the decision.

No cartoon. No sheets. No sale. (For various reasons.) And the dream slowly faded. But the ride. Oh, what a ride. Not to mention, an expensive learning experience.

But I had stuff, 1,300 square feet of stuff. We built the shop when we outgrew the garage. Because we had room, people gave me more stuff, not to mention the stuff left over from Here's the Scoop/Locals Make Good and too many other projects to bore you with. At least my stuff is partly organized now, and I can about see what I have. I almost had myself talked into getting rid of some of it, but I have promised the kids that it is now organized enough that a couple of dumpsters is all it will take—after I'm gone.

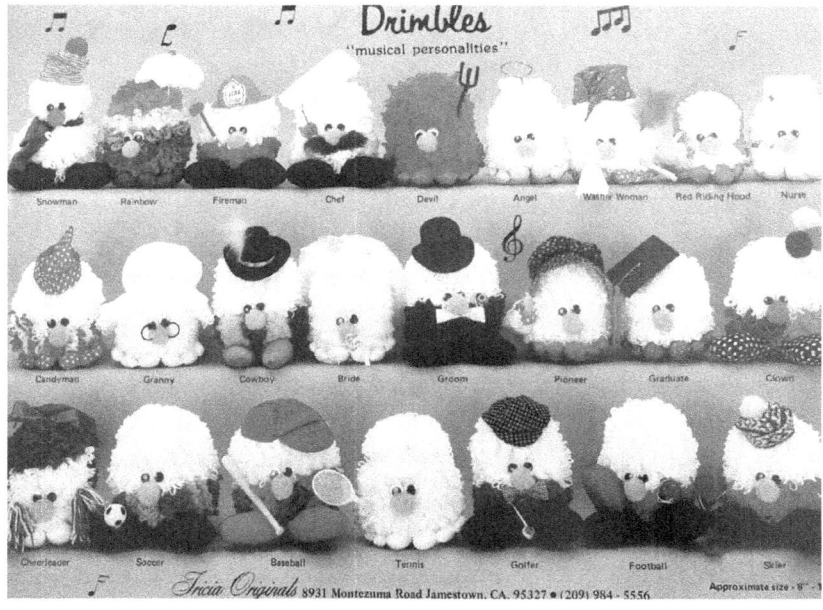

Tricia's Musical Personality Drimbles

Rugs and Drimbles crafted during the COVID lockdown.

Draft 14—November 2021

———— ❋ ————

Are we ever satisfied? Just ran across a note that says, "Now what's the problem? I got a letter. But now it's back to waiting. And more waiting." The next note says, "Mary was right. I do need that instant gratification. This letter-writing is slow. So slow. I wonder how our ancestors survived?"

I imagine I was thinking text versus letter here. Poor me. Poor me. But is it something else entirely? A few days ago, I emailed a few pages of this manuscript to my Write Sister Kirby, hoping she might take a look. She won a Newbery honor, so obviously she knows writing. She said she was flying home to Seattle in the morning and a project like this was perfect for her short plane ride. Then why haven't I heard from her? She hates it. I know she hates it, and simply doesn't know how to tell me. I need to turn my attention elsewhere. Now!

From things you said in your blog, I was ready to be put off by Cohen expecting nothing but crude sexuality in his songs. Your interpretation. All I hear is the same yearning and desire that lurks in all of us, lamenting the despair of non-communication. Was he struggling with what desire has done to the

179

Christian mission? Yearning for love? Drugs? Which leads me to wonder, why is there so much Christian symbolism in Cohen's work? Being raised a Jew? And I have decided it is because all religion, like Broadway, has many good suggestions for ways to surf this life. There are seven billion eight hundred million of us—with all our different ways of thinking and living on this tiny planet. If you are looking for miracles, how about the fact that we still have somewhere to live?

Kirby wrote! Kirby wrote! Took only four days. But she likes where I'm headed. My soul is at peace once more. Until I wonder, where are you? Nothing lasts.

A letter. Nearly six weeks had passed before this short "tentative no." Well, it wasn't a positive no. Now what?

"You and I write a book together? Such an idea! I'm pretty sure my answer is no, but it's fun to think about, and it may give me a boost in my little feud with books."

"Anyway, consider this a tentative no. I wanted to get something in the mail since I've been dawdling so." Of course my attempt to convince him went into the mail the next day. And I waited.

Not quite so long a wait this time. But still no real decision either.

Letter 27: November 2021

---✻---

Will you stop with the books already? There is no way you can read them all, so how can you know all that is out there? And like with the vehicles you are comparing them to, you hear most about the ones people think they want, are interested in. As for OUR book, I've never seen one quite like it, and I read A LOT! But maybe not enough memoirs or biographies to know what is actually out there. Not quite sure what genre this book falls into, but I feel it falls somewhere in between.

Here's the thing: I get it that you aren't quick on the trigger to make a decision. Guess you could say I'm a tad more impulsive, and when I decide to do something, I get to doing. But I now have more than 35,000 words in my first draft, heading for something around 50,000. What I would need from you—if you decide yea—is how my various letters hit you.

Know what the very best thing is about this project? The dam has broken and I'm writing. I had no idea how much I was missing it, and I am not stretching things a single inch when I say that.

Hope you had a nice Thanksgiving. Mine has been fabulous!! Even though I am spending it alone again this year. As you will see if you read the book, there are family issues over the vaccine that I had no desire to deal with. And COVID cases have gone way up in Tuolumne County.

But John brought me ham from our pigs, all sorts of carbs, and homemade bread on an actual china plate. On his way up, he picked up yesterday's mail. And there it was! The focal point of all the letters I have been writing you since my last letter went off. If you would like to read them now, you will have to simply agree to collaborate. If not, I guess you will have to wait until the book is published—like everyone else. Except my Write Sister Kirby. I sent her eighteen pages to see what she thought. She said very nice things and told me to keep writing. Didn't need to push too hard.

Just want to make sure you understand that I will be moving ahead while you try to decide. The book will remain basically the same no matter which way you decide to go. Your input would be delicious frosting on the cake.

BTW, you didn't even bother to tell me if in fact you told JR the same things you told me, way back when.

I could say there is no hurry for a decision, but I really want to know which direction to head. I also want you to understand that this book is basically about me. And because of you, I began my quest.

Do you realize this is the quickest a letter has gotten from you to me in the year and a half we have been corresponding? They usually take 3–4 days. Yes, I check. This one arrived in my mailbox two days after being sent. And it came just in time, since my last draft letter to you warns that I was giving you only two weeks more and that was that.

Ride the wave. Life is what happens while you are making other plans. We are old. What else do we have to do? I guarantee you one thing, you will definitely know more about me once you have read the book.

Letter 28: November 2021

Quick note. It's good! Please! Make a decision. Say yes! I've been typing. It works! If you really want to know what someone is saying in a letter, type it. Feels as though we are already working together. Best of two worlds here, BOTH books and letters. No?

Draft 15—November 2021

— ❋ —

Win, win, win. That's all I seemed to be doing during those weeks I didn't hear from you. Then here came the letter. And there went my winning streak. What does this mean? Maybe I won't be happy with your final decision? Then, when I think it's all over, here I go, sailing right along once more. Win, win, win.

The words banging in my head this morning are "C'est Magnifique-a" (from *Can-Can*). Not good, because the next line goes, "It is so tragic-a." Would you please hurry up and decide? I know. I know. There has barely been enough time for our letters to cross. Have you ever heard of texts? Email? The most difficult part about this, I may not have "become accustomed to your face." How could I when I haven't seen your face in over sixty years? But "Damn! Damn! Damn! Damn!" Lately, "you almost make my day begin." Because I have to play my games to insure your decision. "I was serenely independent and content"—as I'm sure you were—before I began this quest. "Surely I could always be that way again—And yet" (*My Fair Lady)* here I sit waiting, waiting, waiting.

I am still trying to figure out what exactly is going on with me and this family situation. I asked one of my grandsons to stop by yesterday and explain to me why he is anti-vaccine. I really am trying to understand, though I know none of them believe me. One of the things I picked up on is fear of the negatives. All the bad things this vaccine has done to some. But when I asked, what about what COVID has done to the many? It was like I was not listening. They call us vaccine-believers sheep, same as we call *them* sheep. They, too, get their information from the internet, the media—just different sites. We are pushing if we state what we think. But the biggest problem, as I see it, is that they do not like anyone telling them what to do. I remember. I didn't want anyone telling me what to do either at that age. Well, at any age, I guess. I can't say only the young feel this way, but it seems to me it is mostly a grandparent/grandchild contention. And he seemed to take my decision not to host a family celebration this year personally. It's not about him. It is a decision. My decision. Am I really the bad guy for ruining family tradition? He truly believes that if we gather, COVID can simply be another taboo subject, much as we have always handled politics and religion. But unlike most politics and religion, this subject continues to kill people every day. Right here in the U.S.! Right here in Tuolumne County! Can we not try what we have on hand, to see if we can slow it down? And don't give me "the vaccine is too new, there hasn't been enough time for testing." COVID vaccines have been in the works for twenty years. Aren't we simply using a variant on a variant? And every vaccine in the world can be harmful to someone.

He also claims that he no longer feels welcome here. This was especially hurtful as I have never, from the beginning of this pandemic, turned any individual away. My problem is simply with gatherings, the concentration of breaths. Then I wonder... Is it really because of me? Or because of feeling guilty? I have carried enough guilt through the years, earned or not, to recognize the reaction. Another perfect example of them versus us. What surprises me the most is how much more upset he seems to be about our differences. Is this because of the perspective that age offers?

One thing I wish my family would wake up to is that no matter if I decide to have this family gathering to "keep tradition alive" or not, not everyone will gather. Does this, too, fall on my shoulders alone? As for decisions, you have the right to make yours. Don't I have that same right? And we are both dealing with the consequences. There are always consequences.

Here is what I have decided: We, the aging, have walked the walk. Look back and assess what you have accomplished. Is it good overall? Then forgive yourself if you can't fix every little thing. Whether I believe it or not, it is not all about me. How can it be when there are 7.8 billion *me*s in our world?

Talked to my nephew yesterday. He lives in the greater Los Angeles area and does not believe in vaccines either. And he is a generation ahead of my grandchildren. What he has decided is to sell everything he owns in California and move to one of the red states. Wow! Running away to another state to avoid controversy? Talk about them versus us. And we think our last war between the states was bad?

This afternoon there are two woodpeckers out front, each checking their own metal pole on the fence. This tells me that my friend the woodpecker, who was here a couple weeks ago, 'told' someone about his find. Is this what we humans do when we pass ideas along, even such as those that are untrue or may never work?

Draft 16—November 2021

—✤—

It just dawned on me. I keep babbling about my games, and I bet you have no clue what I am talking about, since you only play solitaire and are probably wondering how I can use my morning game-wins as a gauge for how my day might go. As hard as I try, I cannot picture solitaire as a measure of life. But Candy Crush? That's another story. And here is why. In a game, you have no choice but to play the hand dealt to you, as in life. But in life, you—not they—can choose how to play it. Or so many of us believe. Often when you feel ready to throw in the towel, here come all the right moves, and you are flying high once more. You start feeling cocky. The next thing you know, nothing is going your way. You feel anxious. You feel blue. Sound familiar?

Games are also good for anger management. One day, I accidentally hit the wrong move on a play I had been working, which screwed up everything I had so carefully planned. Who cared? My laptop? No, only me. So, you give up, or try again. And again. Then suddenly it happens. You win again. Does this help you understand that eventually things might work the same way in your life if you follow similar procedures? Probably not. We are humans.

I hear it. Loud. Pounding in my head. "Pick yourself up, dust yourself off, and start all over again." (from *Swing Time*)

Then again, no matter how I look at it, losing is losing. Losing by one move, game after game, might be the greatest ego-buster of all, made worse when you seem to have a zillion possibilities that take you nowhere, or so it seems. All those wasted moves are what really drive you crazy. But most of you understands that you simply have to keep playing until they let you win again. Very frustrating when a move you have been working on, and in many cases should do as planned, drops where you want it, only to explode—because they don't want you winning yet. It happens. Believe me!

You know you are close to winning again when bonus offers begin to increase. "Special savings." "Limited time offer." The one that really catches your attention: "77% of players need a boost on this level." Temptation at its best. But I WILL NOT bite. I will show them. I belong in the toppy top, over the 77%. Riiiight.

When bonus moves reach about twenty (in one of the games), you can almost smell a win nearing once more. What does this mean exactly? It means simply that you have played your way through over twenty of the same game. Over. And over. And over. (That doesn't include how many games you have played before the bonuses are increased.) All this to move up one step! How many times have I done this? And there are those who claim I don't focus.

I remember one time not being able to see any strategy that would work. Did I skip that game? You are allowed to skip, but I never have. I decided to keep playing until lives ran out, game after game after game. Have no idea how many days it took to win that game but win I did. If you can call that winning. But sometimes the best strategy is no strategy. Make your moves. Let things happen. They have to line up eventually. Right? Have I mentioned anger management?

I'm beginning to wonder if my need to win games is not simply an indicator that I need a sign that what I think is a great idea *is* a great idea? I do not believe this! Or so I think. But winning brings such hope. As in life, one minute you are up, up, up. The next, everything comes crashing down around you, and you are sure nothing will ever be right again.

A couple mornings ago, nothing was going right. Not only was it a "super-hard game," but none of the moves came anywhere near where they could do any good. The kind of game you want to be over so you can move on...which suddenly got me wondering, is this how you are feeling? You write me a note with a "tentative no," and what do I do? Make my move. Bombard you with reasons. Maneuver for that winning thrust. Me. Me. Me.

Sometimes it feels like I'm knocking on the door to understanding me—if only I can get it open.

Games, like life, need a bit of luck, along with a lot of experience, to be played right. Games are like test-labs as we try over and over to determine what makes what work.

Just realized, I am definitely pitching to you. That my pitches seem out of control falls on your shoulders as I see it. Would I need to work so hard if you would only make a decision? At least a game warns when it's a super-hard level.

I'm not just saying this. I feel games are good for my brain. Game decisions may not be life-shaking, but they are choices. Will playing protect me from Alzheimer's? I doubt it. But it may be good for cognitive skills. Playing may even help to keep our brains plastic if we work at it. Use it or lose it. And what a perfect excuse for wasting all those hours I spend playing games. So, each year free-and-clear from Alzheimer's, my breaths come a bit easier, and I keep on playing.

Noticed that the game I go for first in the morning is the one that challenges me most—frustrates me most. What's up with that?

I keep talking about boosters. Boosters are a game's little helpers, a lot like vaccines can be life's little helpers. Then again, you might think of boosters as money, a way to buy your way, much as money keeps us from being hungry, from being homeless. Both money and boosters are often very hard to come by. Boosters are the little things that help make games easier to win—when you have them, which is rare. Because when you have them, you use them. So you can win. Win. Win. Win. But I have to win. Or I will never reach my goal. I plan to break 2,000 wins on each of my three games. More than halfway there, I'm guessing. Have already gone over 2,000 on one game, and I am at 1,987 on the second, and just hit 1,000 on the third. That alone sounds like a lot of games. I can't even go there.

Draft 17–December 2021

———◆———

My friend Louise and I have decided to cancel our April cruise reservations because of the new COVID variant. Omicron? This is the second cruise we have had to cancel because of COVID. Who would have believed we would still be canceling a year and a half later? It was a difficult decision. The cruise is not until April, but four months seems like forever yet no time in this pandemic environment. And our final payments are due now. Time to decide. Who knows what tomorrow will bring? Of course, we have never known what tomorrow may bring, but we think we do.

What frustrates me is wondering if I will ever travel again. I'm talking about world travel here. I have sneaked in several short road trips throughout, as you know. But only when I weighed conditions: had my vaccines, was around few people who are also vaccinated, etc. The same went for my recent New York trip. We were required to carry proof of vaccination and to wear masks in all public places. But I doubt I would have made the same trip today with COVID cases on the rise and a new, determined variant. Determined to get into us any way it can.

When I was young, our family made several camping trips to Canada. We loved Canada—especially being in another country. Then when I graduated from high school, my dad took the entire family to Ecuador to meet Eulalia's (our exchange student) family. From that time on, I've been hooked. So, in 1985, when Michelle graduated from high school and Jodi was on a softball tour in Australia, I talked Jack into taking our family on the same kind of trip as ours to Ecuador. Just happens that we too had an exchange student—from Australia. When we got back, Jack said, "Enough traveling for a while." Probably shouldn't have started him on one so far from home. But did that deter me? It only took twenty-five years for me to get him on another plane, but after that, he loved foreign travel as much as I did.

To be fair, Jack always loved travel. So long as he could be the pilot, which required places we could drive. And I was an excellent co-pilot, in my opinion. When the kids were young, we even had a motor home. I have lost count of how many times we crossed the United States. Not sure we hit all the National Parks, but it had to be close. For our fortieth anniversary, we drove to the most eastern tip of New Brunswick. The next year, we drove to Fairbanks, Alaska. On that trip, we took the ferry up the inland passage to Valdez. We happened to travel at the same time as many First Nations people were headed for an annual social gathering. What magic! We listened to their lilting conversations and watched as they put finishing touches on their dance capes.

196

Here is how I got Jack to travel overseas with me again: Once our families were grown and we three were all over fifty, my sisters and I began to travel together. To be accurate, the two of them had begun traveling until I could no longer stand it and finally budgeted the time to join them. We can always find the time to do what we want to. Right?

Pam, Tina, and I went first to Ecuador, then South Africa, then Hungary and its surrounding countries. We were in the middle of planning our upcoming trip to Spain when it happened. First, I need to tell you that Jack was highly allergic to what we call the Chinese kissing bug or bedbug. His first attack came the year we moved down to Montezuma, and though no bug was found at this time, it was determined that this is what had caused his racing heart and other symptoms that required calling an ambulance. He was given some sort of allergy medicine to put under his tongue, which he had occasion to do maybe five times. Then nothing happened again—for forty years!

One day, I was making soup at Here's the Scoop when I got the call. I rushed home to find an ambulance and a firetruck with about a dozen first responders in my living room and driveway. Jack was stretched out on the floor and did not look good! He had crawled from his pickup into the house to call 911. He spent that night in the hospital and was sent home the next day. I was shaking out his jeans, after washing them, and what fell to the floor? A Chinese kissing bug. After this, he carried an Epi pen wherever he went. Well, in his pickup anyway. He had two more attacks that we handled easily. Now, back to my sisters.

I was on the phone with Tina deciding where we would meet in Spain. Jack was reading the paper in his chair. He dropped the paper and raised his finger. He was never thrilled when I traveled, so I thought he might be objecting to something I'd said. That's when he passed out. I slammed down the phone and ran to find his Epi. Nothing! I called John and kept looking. Finally, there it was UNDER the console in his truck. I grabbed it, ran back to the living room, and slammed the needle into his thigh, bending needle against bone, just as John came through the door. I told John my story and that his father was fine. John slugged him in the chest. To this day, he claims his father wasn't breathing. A minute later Jack woke up, as though nothing had happened. But here is the good part: I told Jack I was canceling my plans to go to Spain. How could I leave him at such a time? But my canceling came with a price. He had to go to Italy with me. He agreed. He fell in love with the European rail system. We were in Europe four more times. Our last trip, eight months before he died, was with my sister Tina and her husband Brian by train. We hit eleven countries in twenty-four days, from London to Oslo, included tours and side trips, and we all loved every minute. There was no sign of a cough until we got back, and even then, it was not anything particularly noticeable for another six months. I give thanks every day that we had no idea what was to come.

I have now traveled in five of our seven continents. I doubt I will ever see Antarctica. In fact, I don't feel any desire to see Antarctica. I'm not big on snow. But Asia was on my list for our first COVID year. The plan was to take my youngest grandson to Japan. He loves everything Japanese and wanted to tour a samurai sword factory. This would have been my fourth grandchild trip. My first was to New Zealand, Iceland was number two, the Netherlands and France was number three. Plus, my two daughters and I toured Greece where we met up with my exchange sister Eulalia, whose daughter was living in Thessalonica at the time.

I guess what I am trying to get to here is, will I be traveling like this ever again? I can blame it on COVID all I want, but time marches on, as does my wonky heart. Yes, I use your term a lot. Wonky heart. Says it all. I am now thinking I may need to take my remaining three grandchildren on the same trip. Has its pluses and minuses. I'm sure they will have a better time with cousins their age. But I did so enjoy my one-on-one time with each of them.

Draft 18—December 2021

———— ❉ ————

No wonder I like cats. I'm just like them. I only pay attention to what I want to pay attention to. What's important to me at the moment. And they communicate about as well as I do. I don't allow my cats in my bedroom at night. So Silky lets me know how she feels about this. Lately, she goes into the guest bathroom after I close my door and pulls every towel down onto the floor, including the ones that are folded on the back of the toilet. What do you think she's trying to tell me?

That's the thing. I only hear what I want to hear, I am sure. But some quotes stick with me. Forever. In eighth grade, a girl who was in our school only while her father was working in the area said, "Do you know why I don't like you? Because you try so hard to make everybody like you."

In high school, a friend high up on the Rainbow Girls chain said, "You can't be in Rainbow Girls because you have to tell all your secrets to the priest." Huh? Are there still Rainbow Girls?

When I was older, a friend said, "You are a good friend—so long as it is on your terms."

Another said, "You have a Taiwanese soul." This one I liked because she meant I could crank out a lot of stuff.

My favorite: "You can't take constructive criticism," and he seemed quite surprised. Do you know anyone who likes criticism—constructive or not? But what I wonder: why are these the things I remember? Seems like they all track directly to this me thing.

Something else I think about: Why are we so down on embarrassment? Some things I never got wrong again were because of embarrassment. Especially words. I was in my first weeks of college when Sister Gertrude Mary made a huge deal about my pronunciation of epoch. In front of the entire class. Did I ever forget? Not the experience. Not how to pronounce that stupid word. Then I began watching many prehistory programs on YouTube and guess what? The Brits pronounce epoch exactly as I did. Makes me proud.

I know my Write Sisters are happy I am back writing. I know that some of them are also concerned I will be sending out my masterpieces before they are ready—something I have been known to do. Is impulsivity an addiction? Do you think there are things just as addictive as drugs, alcohol, gambling? Such as work, impulsivity, winning?

Is it impulsivity? Or ignorance? So often, you feel you are writing the best thing you have ever written. How long are you supposed to wait to know? Do you ever know? They say, "Put it away for a couple weeks, then look at it again." I've put a lot of it away for more than twenty years, and it still looks good to my eyes. Still sounds good to my ears. Says a lot about me as a writer, I'm thinking.

We still crave that feel-good, no matter how old we grow. The other day when I was working at Rawhide, a guy's bill came to $19.59. I said, "1959, that was a great year." And he said, "Was that the year you were born?" He was serious! I was a freshman in high school that year. Made my day!

A woman came in that same day. We got to talking about travel. I must have mentioned taking my grandchildren on trips because she said she wanted to do that too. She was not quite my age but getting close. Unfortunately, she seemed to be using the theme song so many of us use: "Tomorrow, tomorrow, I'll do it tomorrow"—to skew Orphan Annie's well-known words. That's when another song rings in my head: "Tomorrow never comes," but that's an Elvis thing, not a Broadway song, so maybe we are okay.

Somewhere in this waiting game I realized that if nothing else came from my cajoling, there was something positive going on here. Telling him about my life while I awaited his decision, I was writing my memoir. And having fun doing it. I wanted him in on the project, but the feeling grew stronger each day that I would soon be going it alone. Was that a bad thing? I looked back over our letters. I compared their information, their lengths. Writing them was never a chore to me though I often got the feeling it was to him. So write. Leave him alone. Could I do that? But I still enjoyed our letters crossing paths occasionally.

Draft 19–December 2021

---※---

What if I have to go it alone? Am I wanting your collaboration to keep my backbone strong? Doubt creeps in, the COVID of the mind. Do I doubt I can do it alone? Not really. What's the worst thing that can happen? That I fail? Wouldn't be the first time. And probably not the last. It shows in my knitting. I can put hours into something, and if I don't like it, I'll pull the whole thing out. Can't waste the yarn, can I? To my thinking, that's the sign of a real knitter versus a wannabe. I wish I could share how many times something I have thought was brilliant has failed. Might slow me down. For a while. But usually, I simply binge in another direction. That is the biggest thing this pandemic experience has opened my eyes to. I am not only a binger in eating; I binge everything I do. I don't make a rug, I make RUGS. I don't knit a hat, I knit HATS, or sweaters, or blankets. I don't read a book, I read books (one at a time, of course). I don't make a pie, I make PIES. Notice all the eses? What I haven't figured out is why.

It just seems it would make the book more fun, and probably much more interesting, if you had an active role in it. What do you think works better? Two people pitching, catching, pitching, catching, as the entire world looks on? Or one person tossing the ball into the air, missing most of her catches, at times smashing herself in the face, as she entertains...herself?

That's the thing about writing—no matter how many people you imagine out there absorbing all you have to say, it's about you. You are talking to you. That's why to me, it makes no difference if you are writing a letter or a book. That's why as hard as I have tried, I still don't get what you see as a difference between writing a letter or writing a book. Just like me, my cat talks to herself. The only difference, she doesn't seem to have any desire to write it down.

Doubt. Doubt. The cancer of our soul. Be gone. Forty years ago, I thought I would be dead within the month, yet I have overcome. No matter what nature has thrown my way, I have overcome. I have had my vaccines, my booster. I have overcome. So far. So, what's the challenge in writing a book 125 times longer than the picture books I've been used to? Nothing! It's the words I love to play in, whether they be few or many—it takes what it takes. How many words does it take to paint the picture you see in your mind? Which words do you need to make your picture just right? How could I have given up writing for twenty-five years?

Something else I learned from my games: challenges get tougher the higher you go. Is this the same in life? For some, it definitely is. But does this mean I should have avoided getting back to writing? I now realize I was worried I was too old for marketing. Now here it is six years down the road, and I have forgotten the problem. One of the benefits of age. Once I asked and answered myself, *do you only write to publish?* And I

205

heard in my head a resounding NO. I realized, what did it matter if I died without publishing another thing? Would I care? I can't know yet. But we should always ride the waves until we can't.

So here are the best things about writing: I do not need a 1,300-square-foot shop to store stuff. Words are already in my head. The ones I can still catch anyway. You can do it anywhere. You can write while you are cooking. You can write while you are cleaning your house. You can write while you are driving. The only thing you MUST remember is to put butt to chair once in a while and type out that which has been building in your head. Saves on exploding heads. I find that some of my best writing comes while playing games or just as I'm drifting off to sleep. A real pain either way, because you have to push pause so you can jot down your latest brilliant idea before you forget. Did I mention the problems of aging? Now you have screwed up either your game or your sleep.

We all like to be able to say we are a published author. By a real publisher. I already have a few published books tucked in my belt. But is that good enough? Unfortunately, it's been twenty-two years since my last book came out. So, no matter how much I fight it, there seems to be something whispering in there somewhere that I am a failure because I haven't published in twenty-two years, no matter that I haven't written in the same twenty-two years.

Just like Jack put the brakes on me by buying that building, knowing I would come out of my writing once I got caught up in a fun new project (and how right he was). COVID seems to have flipped the switch. Would I have gone on crafting, reading, traveling, if not for COVID? If not for my quest? Like it or not, you are one of the reasons I am back in my happiest of places. It began with these simple letters. Over and over, I harp on life being what happens while you are making other plans, to look for the good no matter how bad the bad. But am I satisfied?

P.S. How many times has one of your letter writers told you that they lost their train of thought because they had to go put in a dozen piglets that had dug their way onto the highway? It was a first for me, too. We have never had pigs get out before. It's been raining a lot up here lately. Pigs love the muck. So, under the fence they dug, and off they went. Looking for an adventure. And, of course, it had to be when John was on his way to Arizona to pick up equipment. How we all made it out alive, I have no idea. A lady stopped to help. But she fell, scraping her nose in the gravel, which did not help. One bit! Do you think cars would slow down, even with us waving our arms and shouting? I remember telling you earlier that we now truck our cattle across a two-lane road. For this very reason! Grandson Jack came to the rescue. Rounding up piglets on his trusty steed—his four-wheeler. Soon all the pigs squeezed back in to whence they came, and Jack secured the fence. I give thanks that all ended well. With a special thanks that this happened during daylight. I am way too old to be chasing after pigs in the dark. Today I have earned my nightly beer. Stay well.

Letter 29: December 2021

———— ❉ ————

Thank you for your decision even if it is not what I wanted to hear.

I have rarely felt comfortable talking about what I am writing until I have finished it. This book has been different from the beginning, and now I'm wondering why. Has it been to cushion my disappointment? Has it been because I thought if I talked about it, it would be sure to happen as I planned? Is it because all my other books have been drawn from my imagination while this one is very much about my life? I don't know. Maybe because I was looking for approval for what I had planned? Maybe because it was so different from anything else I have ever written. And I have written hundreds of things. Just never a book this long.

Herein lies the problem. I'm a tight writer. Is that why I hoped so much that you would join me? To fill in the holes? But I shall persevere because that is how I am. I HAVE to finish. Be it game or rug or book. Well, that may not be exactly true. Examples of which can be found in my almost-finished rug box, in my almost-finished garment box, in my almost-finished manuscript first drafts file. But this book, I will finish! Even if it is nothing more than another something my children have to deal with after my passing. It will have a beginning, a middle, and an end. It will be done! As will all those things in my almost- finished boxes—one of these days.

When I went in for my annual, I mentioned this book. Dr. Basi listened and smiled. She seemed to like what she heard. As I was leaving, she said, "Hope you finish your book before Christmas." A strange thing to say. Then I thought about it being so much longer than what I normally write and doubted there was a chance. But here I am, with only a couple weeks to go. Can I do it?

She also said, "Always stay as young as you are." Not sure what that meant, but I liked it. Which leads to my final challenge. I'm making a list, checking it twice. Ready or not, here I come. But am I ready? Ready to face me?

Here is what is to me the most major of changes in aging, aside from saggy skin and brain burps: It is how what-is-important changes so much between 17 and 77.

I cannot think of much in my life that I have been afraid of, except maybe the fear of something bad happening to someone I love. Nothing like my mother's lifelong fear of lizards. But I have watched this change inch by inch. Alzheimer's and heights now make me nervous. Heights have rarely worried me my entire life, but now at times I feel the stomach-flips brought on by heights and think I have figured out what is going on. Falling is not a good thing. We aging are not so quick on our feet anymore. I'll bet there is a study somewhere that will show that this is simply another part of human evolution.

Caution. After all, "Prevention is worth a pound of cure." (I have no idea where this comes from.)

Draft 19–December 25, 2021

———— ✸ ————

Thinking of you this morning. It's Christmas and the book is nowhere near done.

You are probably spending Christmas alone, as am I. Heart-wrenching. At the same time, so satisfying. I do love the holidays but have not missed the craziness of the season one bit this year. Though I am ready to get back to what we used to consider normal. Holiday chorales fill the air behind me. Not the popular ones. These seem filled with the promise that this season was originally meant to bring. And I feel at peace.

While I continued to await your decision, I recognized that it would be pivotal for me. In many ways, it excited me. I could not understand how afraid some people are of diving in. They try to find answers to everything before the question is even asked. Am I the fool? I want the road to take me where it will. The more detours, the better. Of course, we need to proceed with caution. But is this any different from how we should live our daily lives? Or is that just me?

What about you? I gave little thought to how my intrusion might play in your sixty years of life-building. To me, the sidebars of life are the seasoning. I guess I thought that is what I was bringing to you. Did I once consider how something similar would strike me? Maybe. Sadly, I will probably never know.

This has been a learning curve for me. Fantasies are not truths. What we see as an adventure, fun, might be nothing more than stress to our target. If this journey has been for me to learn, I think I have. A little. Who says you can't teach an old dog new tricks? So many times over this past year and three-quarters I have felt I have overstepped, that I would never hear another word from you. You warned me from the beginning, no "till death do us part." But being self-centered, I wanted to keep things on my track. I loved finding those letters in my mailbox. I loved the times you thanked me for the thinking my words generated. We so often seemed to be on the same page. And when we weren't, it was all the more fun.

We are not what my imagination had built of us sixty years ago. What I remember is an overall feeling of enjoyment, pride being your girlfriend, of that sixteen-year-old feeling. Of love? Of course. I was sixteen! I do not remember one date. And neither do you. But I know I remember more than you do. Makes me think I should be content that you remember my name. And that, most likely, is because you remember my mother's voice.

I haven't remained inactive as I await your decision. I've been combing the internet, trying to figure out how much things have changed since I was active in publishing because I have decided I want to at least try to market 'our' book. With or without you.

Wow! Have things changed. Where are all the publishers? I have never had an agent, but it looks to me like you have no chance in hell if you don't have one today. So I studied, watched YouTube, then sent out queries to a few who seemed like a good fit, while I waited to hear from you. Quick and nice responses, but no interest. And why should there be? How many years do I have left? How can I benefit their careers? They are all so young. And there are so many talented up-and-comers to choose from.

Now what?

Draft 20–January 2022

───────── ❖ ─────────

It's a new year. COVID did exactly what they said it would do; it killed many people during the holidays and made many more very sick. Am I feeling smug because I was right? Not really. We win a few. We lose a few. Your letter finally got here. I now knew I had lost you as a collaborator. No big surprise there, but it left me with a slightly heavy heart, not only because I now had to come up with a new approach.

This morning was a time to think back to the beginning of this quest. Again, I swear, my intentions were innocent. Or were they? Are intentions ever innocent? What I was looking for was adventure, something to keep me occupied during our forced isolation.

Now it is my turn to thank you. For this adventure. For the thinking. And for pushing me back into writing though you had no clue you were doing it. Neither did I at the time.

A couple weeks ago, I slipped back into afib. It was an entire week before I was cardioverted. It lasted seventeen days. The next time, the cardioversion lasted five hours. So, they did it again the next day. Worked again. Always makes me happy when it takes because I can't help but remember that two-month spell that will never be at the top of my fun list.

This cardioversion has now held for over a week. But the best part was the quick recovery time. I spent a couple days in the hospital while they adjusted my medicines, then spent a few more days with a very mushy brain while my body adjusted to the increase. But here's the thing: because I could do nothing else, I spent hours watching paleoanthropology on YouTube. Then there it was, a zillion how-to videos on indie (independent) publishing. Another present from my friend Fate. Or simply my mushy brain? I haven't a clue. All I know is that none of my Write Sisters are into indie, so this quest will be my own.

Another quest. Will this free you up? I hope not. I've become accustomed to your words, even if they are few and far between. But you never know, maybe this new quest will take the burden of me off of you, though I would never count on it. Know what else? I have also found something to replace Candy Crush. No matter how philosophical I get about what I learn in the zillion hours spent playing my games, they are still considered "wasted" hours by some. Imagine that. I have now discovered DuoLingo. A justifiable waste. Never too late to improve all those years of high school Spanish. Who knows? Maybe I will soon be fluent and can then move on to Navajo or Irish. DuoLingo teaches those too. The program is fun and fast. They offer great incentives which, yes, they also sell. But you can also earn what you need by practicing. Right up my alley. I love that you have a choice other than waiting for the hearts you need to play. And there are still people way better than me. Can I maybe beat a few?

So, what have I learned about me? It's time to quit blaming. What I am is not my parents' fault, not my husband's fault, not even my fault. I am simply a compilation of things I chose to pull close throughout this journey we call life. It is simply what I have chosen to make my right—what's right for me. I see what this quest has done for me, and I can't help but wonder, has it changed anything for you? Has it changed how you view your life, the world?

This morning, I give thanks for that first letter that eventually showed up in my mailbox and your words: "Till death do us part, I don't know." I remember chuckling. Now I wonder, why not? How many more years do we have? You add something to my life. Have no idea how to explain what that is, but it is something I would miss. Very much. One thing I do know: I am no longer the giddy schoolgirl who began this quest. I am now a serious writer. Riiiiiiiiight. But there is so much I want to try. Why did it take six years between closing my store and now to realize that you are never too old, that it is never too late to write? Were those wasted years? No. Look where I landed. Stay well. I will always be waiting for that next letter.

The End

Acknowledgements

A special thanks to my editor Jessica Hammerman who tried hard to keep me on track.

About the Author

———— ❖ ————

Tricia Gardella's books are mostly influenced by the ranch life she stepped into sixty years ago. She writes children's books about ranch animals, ranch routines, and ranch relationships, though occasionally getting side-tracked to explore the myriad other sides of life. She has tried it all, and almost mastered some: canning, cooking, knitting and other fiber arts, rug-making, gardening, and various business ventures. But writing is her happiest of places and she is thrilled to be back after a twenty-year sabbatical. She has a BA in Ancient History and Classical Archaeology, three children, seven grandchildren, and three great-grandchildren, all giving her much food for thought. She lives with two self-centered cats in Central California. *The Quest* is her only attempt at writing for adults.

Tricia Gardella at her desk during the COVID lockdown.

Mama Pig and her little ones say goodbye!

\

www.ingramcontent.com/pod-product-compliance
Lightning Source LLC
Chambersburg PA
CBHW071321120626
46546CB00002B/392